The LEGO® Adventure Book

Cars, Castles, Dinosaurs & More!

For years, I've wanted to learn to be a better builder, to do more with the LEGO bricks I have been creating with my entire life. So today, I decided to do it. I packed up my stuff and headed into the unknown. What will I build? What other LEGO builds might I encounter? It's going to be fun finding out!

Megan Rothrock

no starch press

San Francisco

Printed in China

Fifth printing

18 17 16 15 14   5 6 7 8 9 10

ISBN-10: 1-59327-442-4
ISBN-13: 978-1-59327-442-9

Publisher: William Pollock
Production Editor: Serena Yang
Cover Design: Chris Long
Interior Design: Megan Rothrock
Developmental Editor: William Pollock
Copyeditors: Serena Yang and Riley Hoffman
Proofreader: Alison Law

For information on distribution, translations, or bulk sales, please contact No Starch Press, Inc. directly:
No Starch Press, Inc.
245 8th Street, San Francisco, CA 94103
phone: 415.863.9900; fax: 415.863.9950;
info@nostarch.com; http://www.nostarch.com/

Library of Congress Cataloging-in-Publication Data
Rothrock, Megan.
  The LEGO adventure book : cars, castles, dinosaurs & more! / by Megan Rothrock.
     pages cm
  ISBN-13: 978-1-59327-442-9
  ISBN-10: 1-59327-442-4
  1. LEGO toys. 2. Models and modelmaking. I. Title.
  TS2301.T7R82 2012
  688'.1--dc23
                        2012033902

CONTENTS

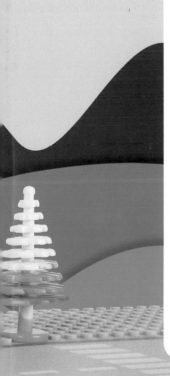

Chapter 1	Building the Idea Lab	4
Chapter 2	A LEGO Town	28
Chapter 3	Hot Rods and Cool Rides	50
Chapter 4	From Below!	56
Chapter 5	The Sky's the Limit	68
Chapter 6	The Turtle Factory	82
Chapter 7	Starfighters	90
Chapter 8	Mighty Mecha	102
Chapter 9	Medieval Village	120
Chapter 10	Triassic Park	134
Chapter 11	Making New Friends	156
Chapter 12	Full Steam Ahead	166
Chapter 13	Steampunk	182
Chapter 14	A LEGO Legend	190

Building the Idea Lab

BEFORE I BEGIN MY TRAVELS, I'LL NEED TO SET UP MY HOME BASE FIRST. I'LL CALL IT THE IDEA LAB!

1

2

Building Tip
Make sure your hinge plates are aligned correctly. This allows the final building to open.

3

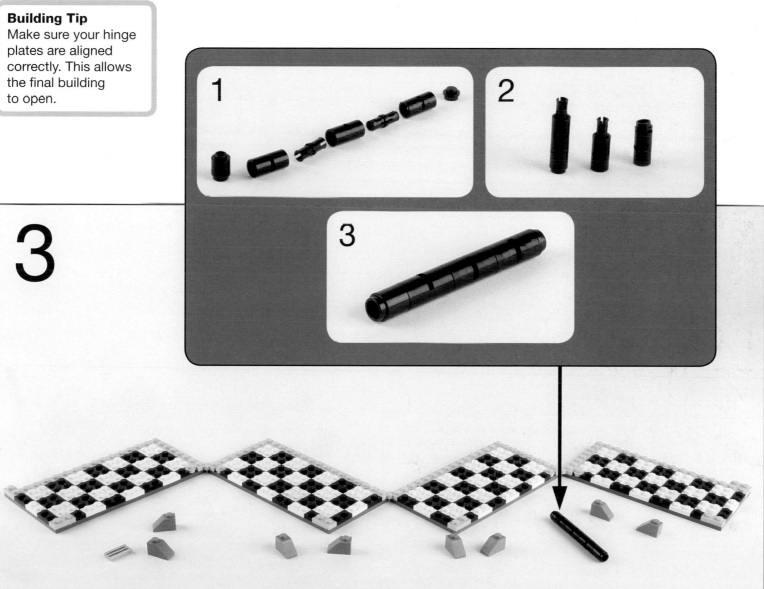

1

2

3

4

5

6

7

8

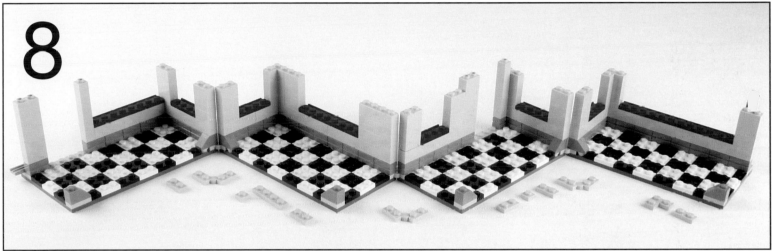

9

10

11

12

13

14

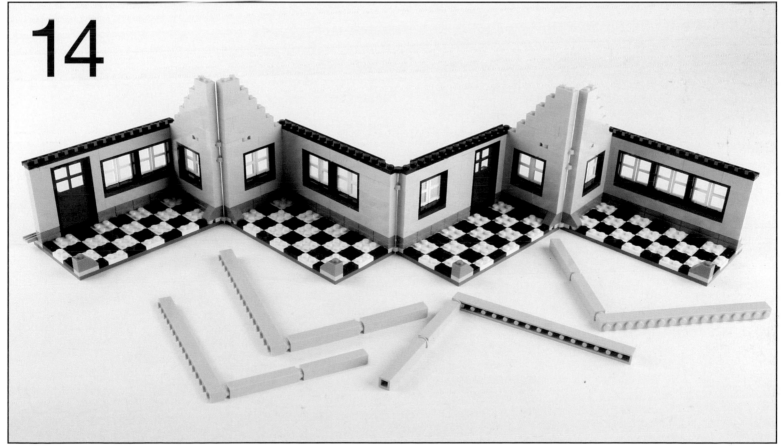

15

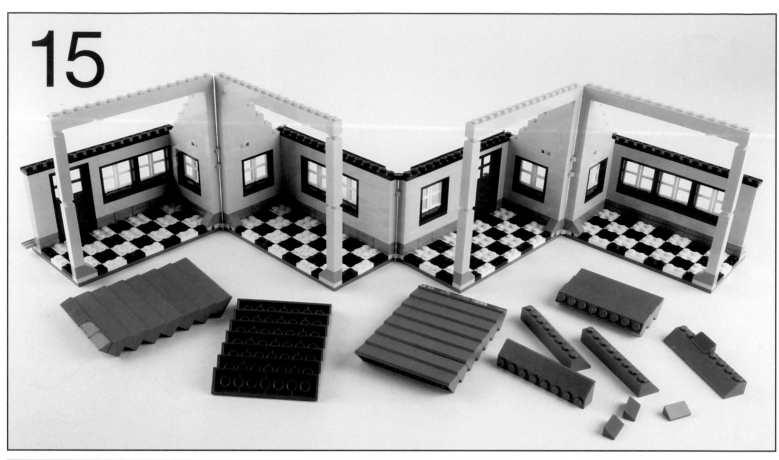

16

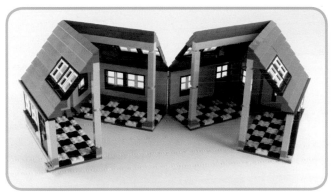

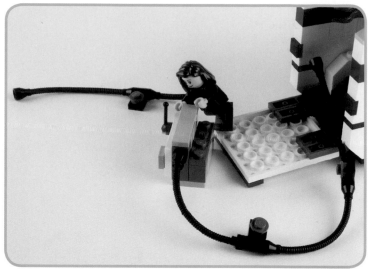

COOL! TURNS OUT I HAVE EVERYTHING I NEED AND THE KITCHEN SINK.

I STILL HAVE A LOT TO DO. I NEED AN ASSISTANT—AND I KNOW JUST HOW TO BUILD HIM!

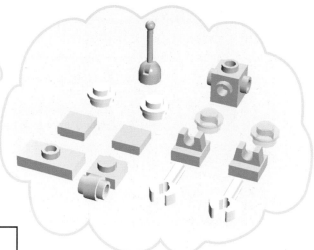

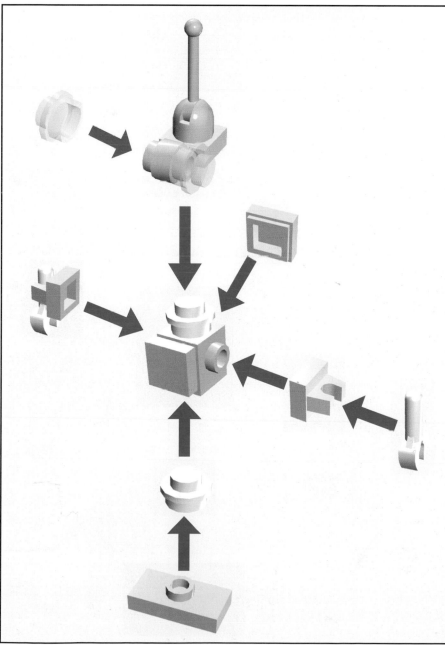

Boot sequence Initiated. Power on. New Grey test complete.

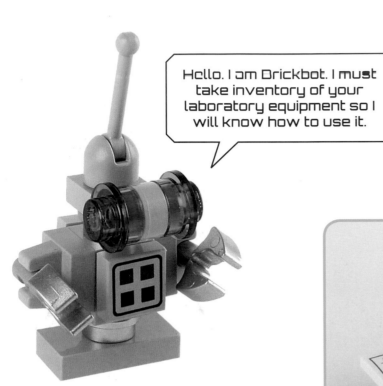

Hello. I am Brickbot. I must take inventory of your laboratory equipment so I will know how to use it.

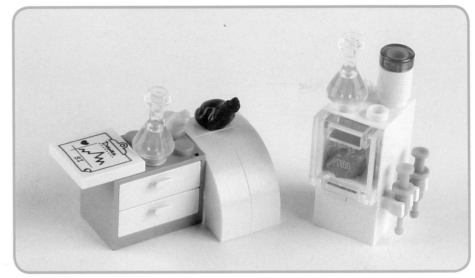

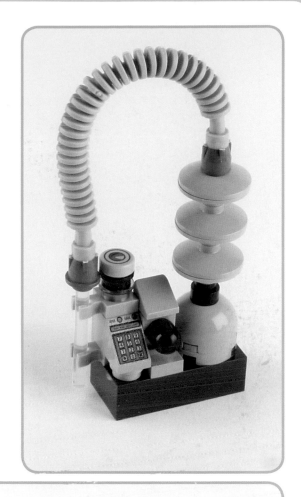

A chair and a lamp?
I do not require
these items.

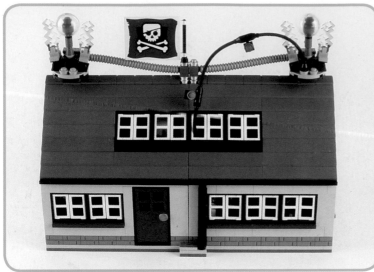

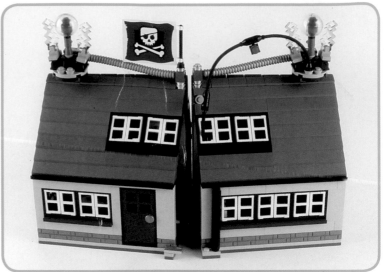

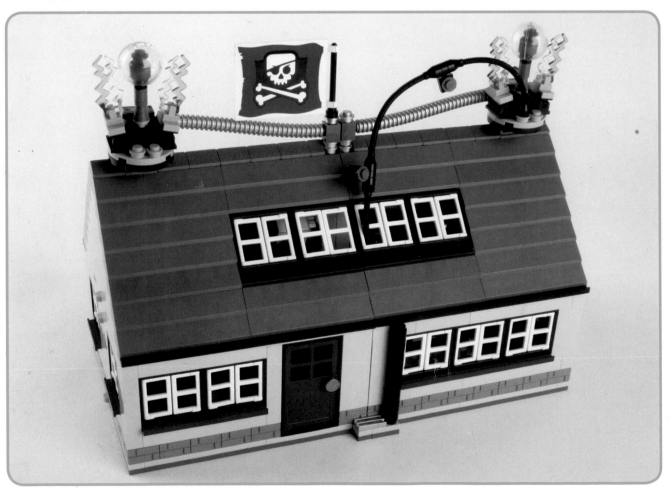

Transport-o-lux

AWESOME! WITH THE POWER COILS IN PLACE, MY AMAZING IDEA LAB IS NOW COMPLETE. I'VE GOT A FEW IDEAS, BUT FOR INSPIRATION I WANT TO SEE WHAT OTHER PEOPLE ARE BUILDING! EVEN THOUGH MY TRUCK IS COOL, I'M GOING TO NEED SOMETHING A LITTLE FASTER.

1

2

3

4

5

6

7

8

ALL FINISHED!

4×4 Truck

BUILDING JOURNAL

As I was working on the Transport-o-lux today,
I remembered my first creation: my 4×4 truck. It
was just in my head one morning, and I had to
build it.

I knew the secrets of building a car, like getting
the right distance between the wheels; making
a good chassis; making the front look right; and
adding lights, a fender, side mirrors, and wheel
arches. I wasn't a vehicle expert, but building my
truck gave me experience with the basics. From
that day on I knew I was a creator—one of the
special ones who can think of a thing and then
build it!

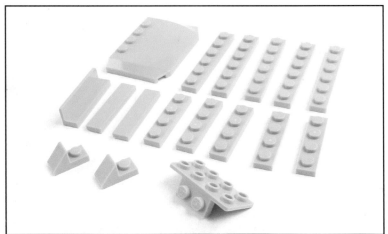

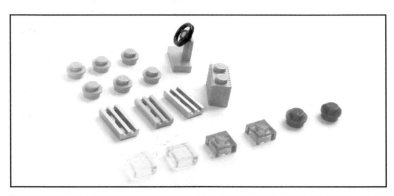

1

2

3

4

5

6

7

8

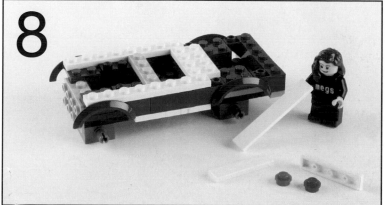

9

10

11

12

13

14

15

16

17

18

19

20

Trailer

MY NEW TRUCK WAS ABSOLUTELY EPIC, BUT IT DIDN'T HAVE ROOM FOR ALL MY STUFF. SO I DECIDED TO ADD A TRAILER!

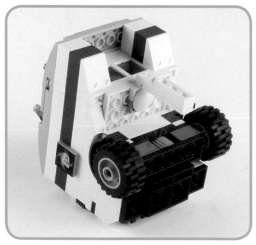

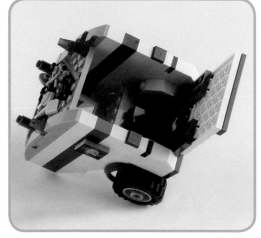

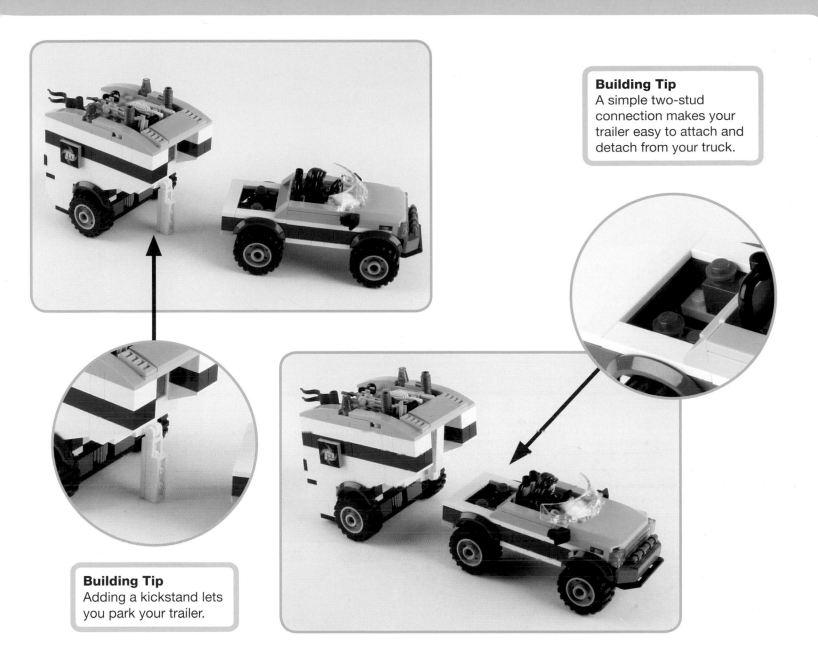

Building Tip
A simple two-stud connection makes your trailer easy to attach and detach from your truck.

Building Tip
Adding a kickstand lets you park your trailer.

BUILDING JOURNAL

I had to think about my trailer's purpose and then add the appropriate details, just like I did with my science equipment.

Adding a trailer can change the look and utility of a vehicle. Now my 4×4 truck can carry much more! I think I'll call it my Idea Truck.

Now that I know which pieces I need for the Idea Truck, I can build it in other colors, too.

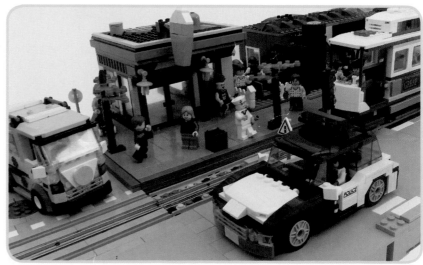

A LEGO Town

Craig Mandeville

Nickname: Solitary Dark

Profession: Aircraft Parts Manager

Nationality: British

Website: *www.flickr.com/photos/36416029@N06/*

HI, I'M MEGS. WHERE AM I?

HI MEGS. I'M CRAIG, AND THIS IS MY TOWN. THAT'S AN INTERESTING VEHICLE YOU HAVE THERE.

THANKS. I BUILT IT MYSELF SO I COULD EXPLORE.

I LIKE TO TRAVEL, TOO. I ALWAYS TAKE MY CAMERA WITH ME AND TAKE LOTS OF PICTURES SO I CAN BUILD WHAT I SEE ON MY TRIPS.

I SAW A CABLE CAR LIKE THIS IN SAN FRANCISCO. I'LL SHOW YOU HOW I BUILT IT.

Cable Car

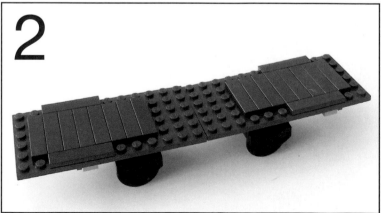

3
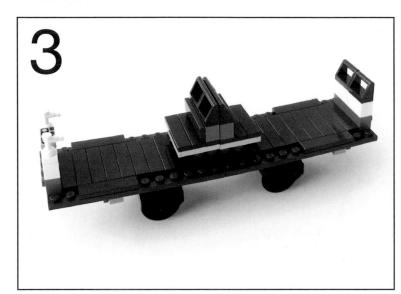

4

5
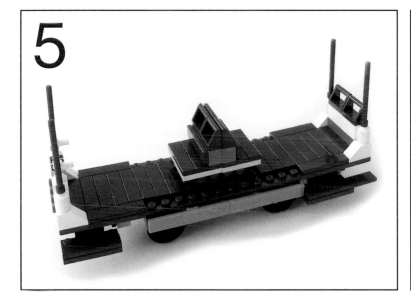

6

7

8

9

10

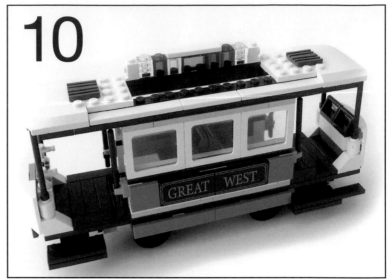

11

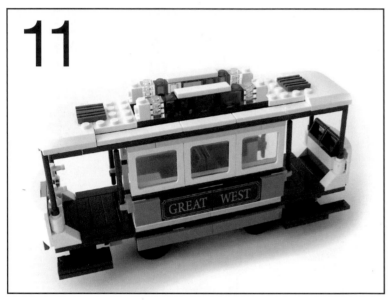

12 ×2

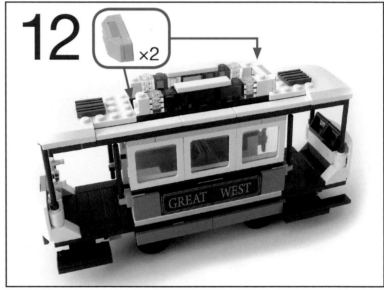

13

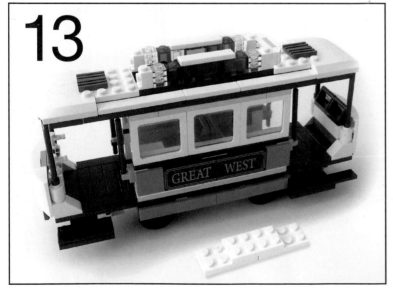

14

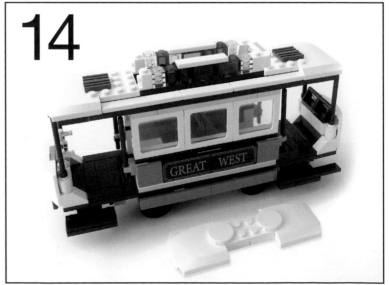

CERTAINLY! THIS IS A GREAT EXAMPLE OF HOW TO BUILD A SMALL SHOP. IT'S A COFFEE SHOP, BUT YOU CAN CREATE ANY KIND OF SHOP YOU'D LIKE. MAYBE A CANDY SHOP FILLED WITH CANDY!

Coffee Shop

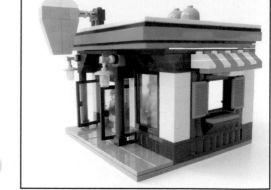

1

2

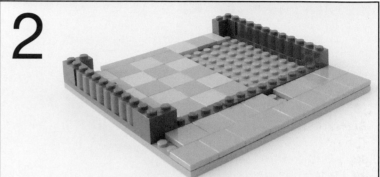

3

4

5

6

7

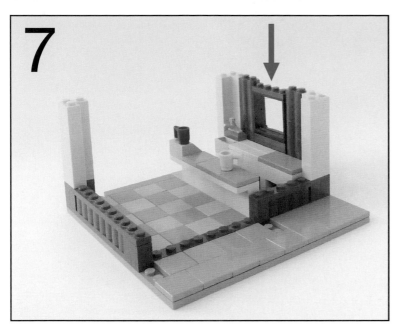

Building Tip
The sides of this building and
some of the slopes on this model
are unstable until locked in place.

8

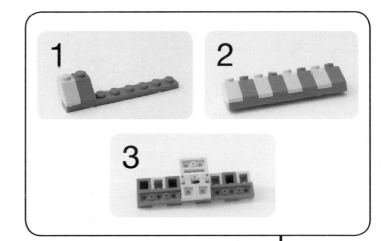

1

2

3

9

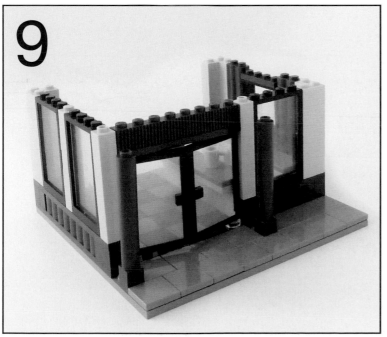

10

11

12

13

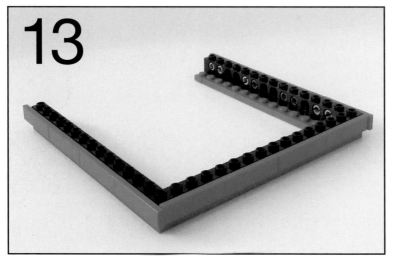

14

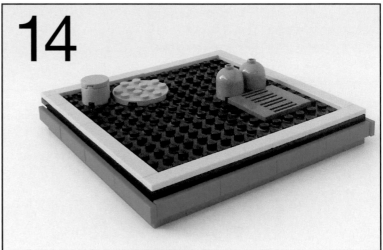

15

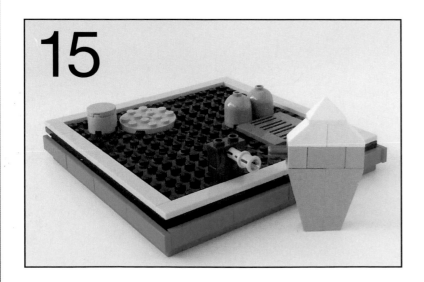

BUILDING JOURNAL

Craig has a way of subtly changing a few details to make each of his buildings unique and iconic. The window styles, the colors, and the sign outside say that this is a coffee shop. I have to remember how important these details are!

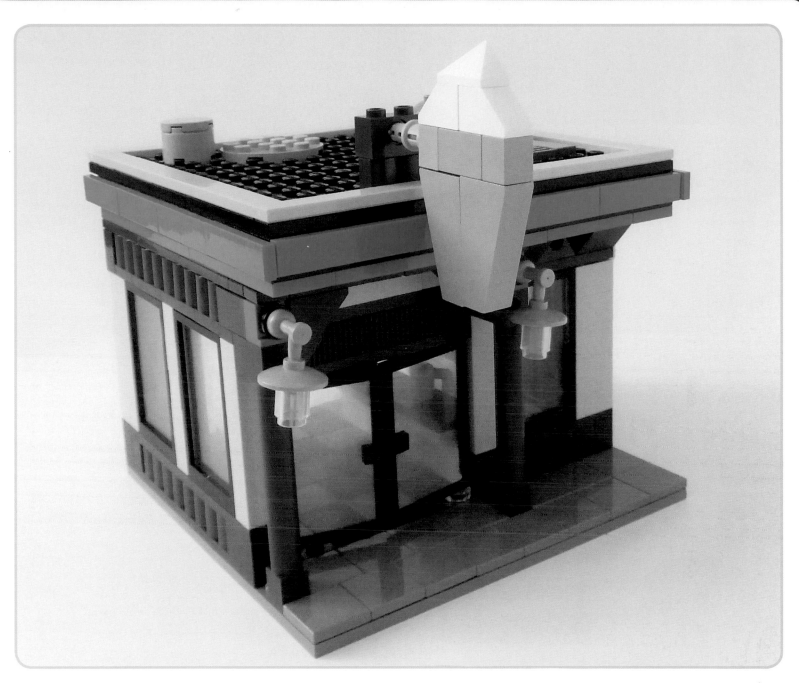

BRILLIANT! IF I CHANGE THE COLORS AND SOME OF THE DETAILS, I CAN BUILD ANY TYPE OF SHOP!

EXACTLY! OKAY, LET'S EXPLORE MORE OF MY TOWN!

HERE IS ANOTHER ONE OF MY FAVORITE PLACES: THE ZOO. YOU CAN BUILD ANYTHING WITH LEGO BRICKS.

THAT'S TRUE, BUT WHEN YOU'RE BUILDING SOMETHING SO LARGE, WHERE DO YOU START?

WELL, LET'S PICK SOMETHING SMALL, LIKE MY ZOO BUGGY OVER THERE.

Zoo Buggy

BUILDING JOURNAL

Tire choice is important for vehicles. Use smooth tires for racing cars and electric vehicles like Craig's Zoo Buggy.

3

4

5

6

THIS BRIDGE IS ANOTHER SMALL MODEL THAT YOU CAN ADD TO ANY SCENE.

Bridge

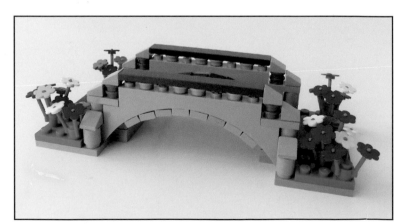

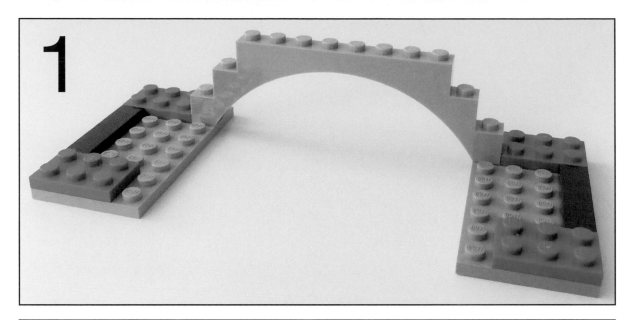

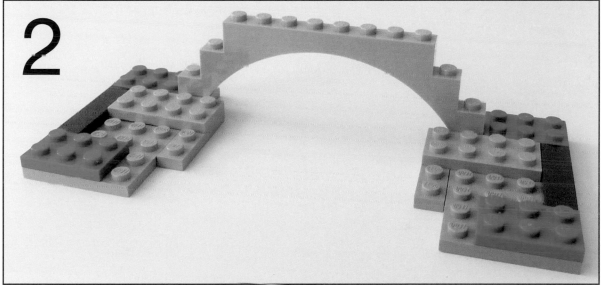

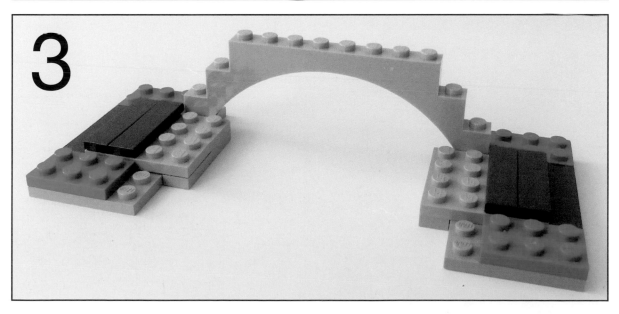

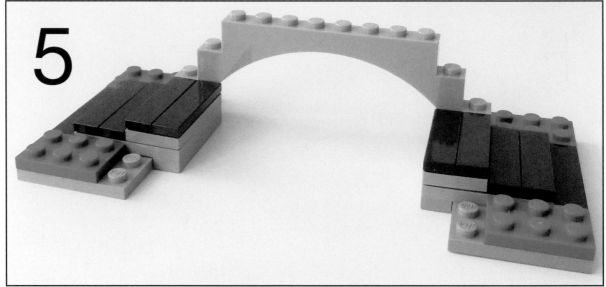

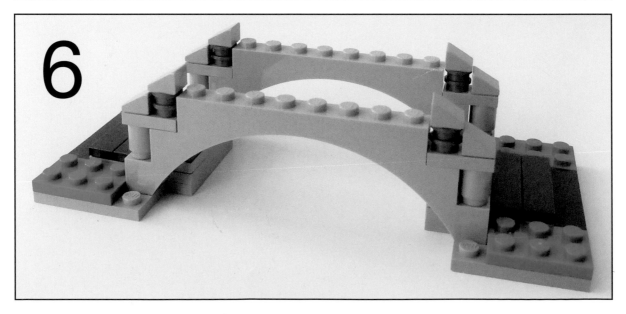

7

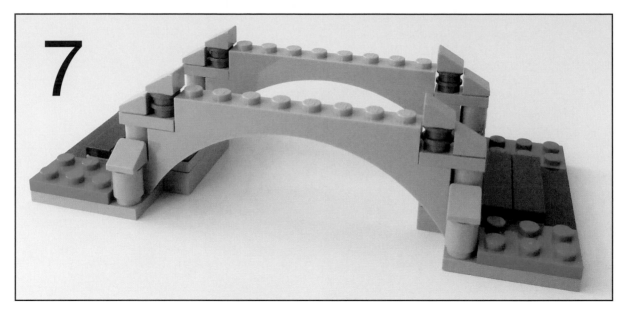

8

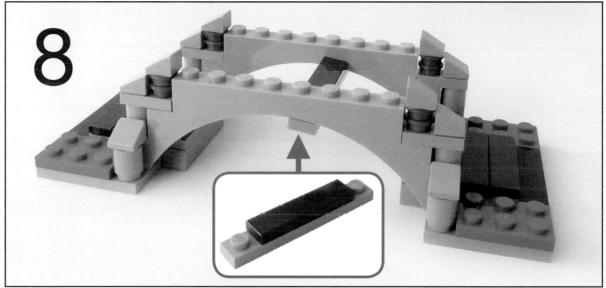

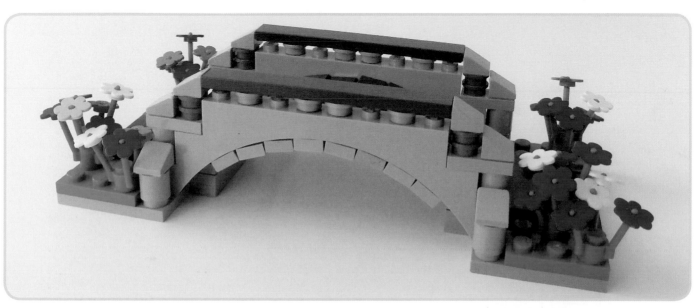

HERE'S A HOUSE. WITH JUST A FEW CHANGES TO THE WINDOWS AND DOORS— AND A DIFFERENT COLOR SCHEME—THIS COULD BE A BAKERY OR A CAFÉ.

OF COURSE, EVERY TOWN NEEDS A GARAGE, AND THIS ONE HAS PLENTY OF VEHICLES TO BE SERVICED. WATCH OUT FOR THE CAT, THOUGH!

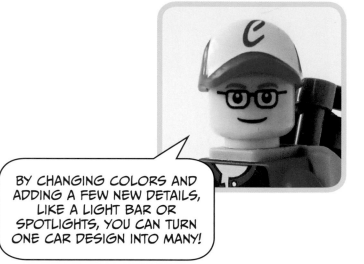

BY CHANGING COLORS AND ADDING A FEW NEW DETAILS, LIKE A LIGHT BAR OR SPOTLIGHTS, YOU CAN TURN ONE CAR DESIGN INTO MANY!

WOW, CRAIG! THANKS FOR SHOWING ME HOW TO BUILD SOME OF YOUR BEAUTIFUL LEGO TOWN MODELS. I HAVE SOME GREAT IDEAS NOW!

YOU'RE WELCOME, MEGS. COME BACK AND VISIT ANYTIME. I LOOK FORWARD TO SEEING THE MODELS YOU COME UP WITH.

WILL DO. DO YOU KNOW ANY OTHER CAR BUILDERS? I'D LIKE TO LEARN MORE!

YOU SHOULD VISIT ARE. I'VE HEARD HE MAKES SOME AMAZING CARS.

ALRIGHT! I'M ON MY WAY!

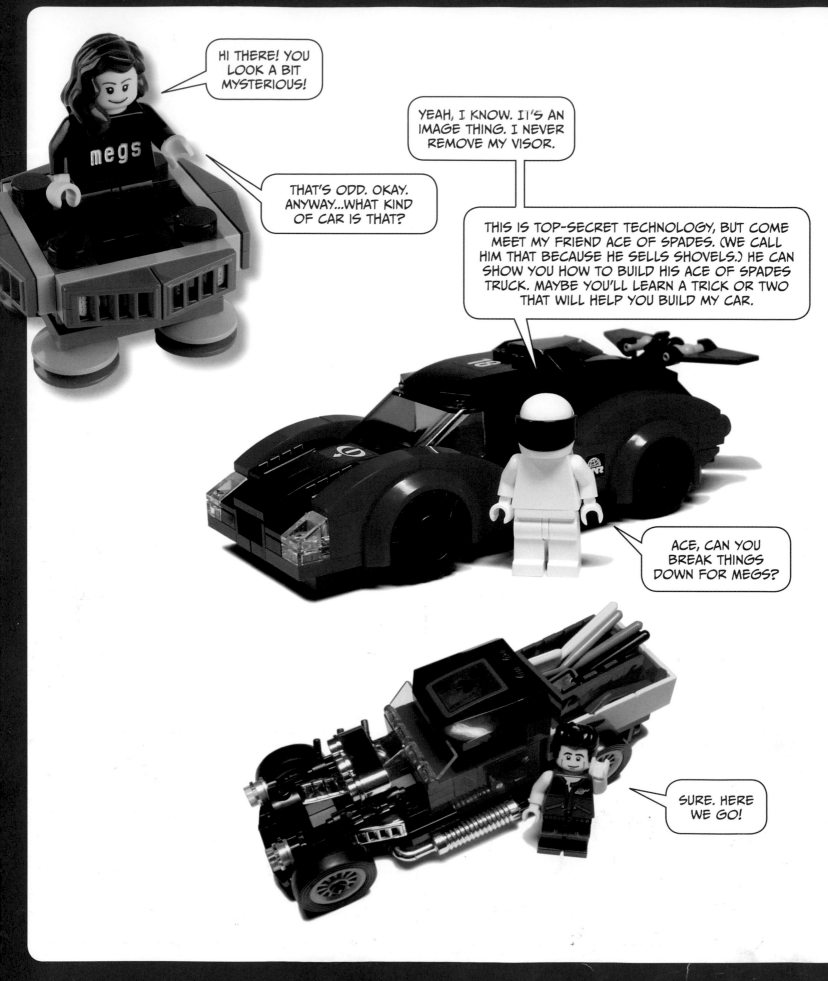

Hot Rods and Cool Rides

Are J. Heiseldal

Nickname: L@go

Profession: TV Journalist

Nationality: Norwegian

Website: *www.flickr.com/photos/legolago/*

Ace of Spades

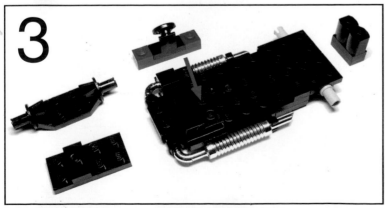

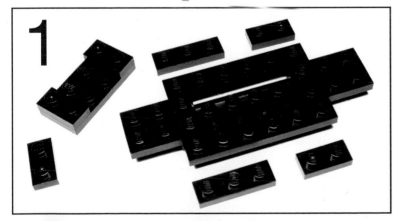

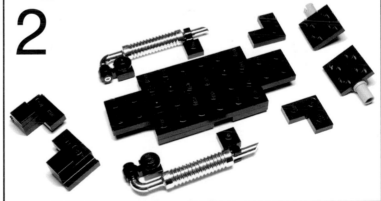

5

XFVXDLST

6

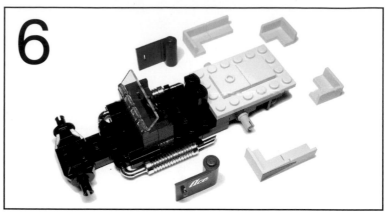

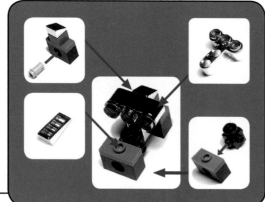

7

8

9

MY TRUCK IS READY TO ROLL!

Building Tip
You can add more character to your vehicles by decorating them with stickers, like the ones on the Ace of Spades truck.

LET ME SHOW YOU SOME OTHER SWEET RIDES.

BUILDING JOURNAL

Are's cars have lots of engine details. Before building my car, I think I'll put aside a few small elements and see if I can build an engine block that will fit in my design. Hot rods tend to have exposed engines so you can see their craftsmanship. Sports cars cover their engines with smooth, curved hoods so they'll go faster!

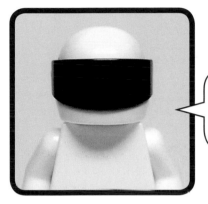

NICE WHEELS, ACE. HERE ARE SOME OF MY SUPERCARS READY TO RACE.

WHOA! WHAT'S THAT RUMBLING SOUND?!

From Below!

FAIR WARNING, BUILDING THE JACKKNIFE IS NOT EASY. LET'S START BY BUILDING THESE FOUR SMALL MODULES.

Jackknife

1

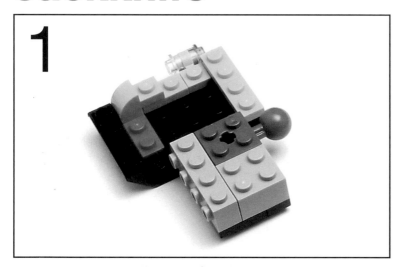

2

3

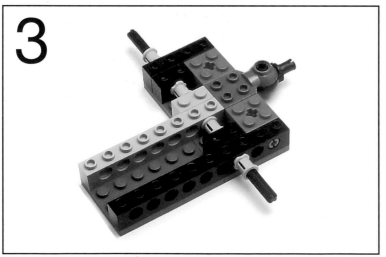

4

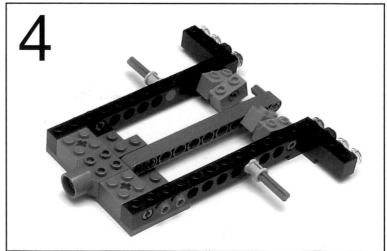

Moritz Nolting

Nickname: nolnet

Profession: Creative Director

Nationality: German

Website: *www.flickr.com/photos/nolnet/*

5

LAY OUT THE MODULES LIKE THIS AND KEEP BUILDING UP EACH OF THEM SEPARATELY. THEY WILL ALL CONNECT IN STEP 10.

6

7

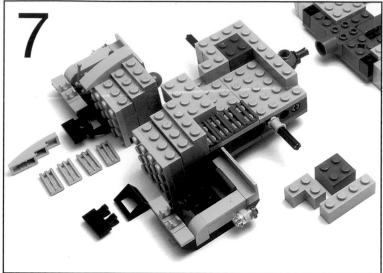

EVEN THOUGH WE BUILT THESE MODULES IN STEP 7, THEY AREN'T ATTACHED TO THE JACKKNIFE UNTIL LATER.

8

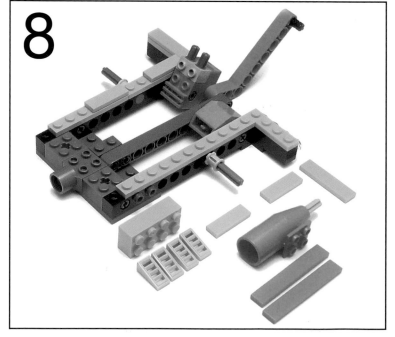

9

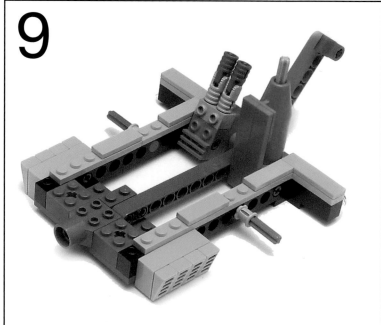

10

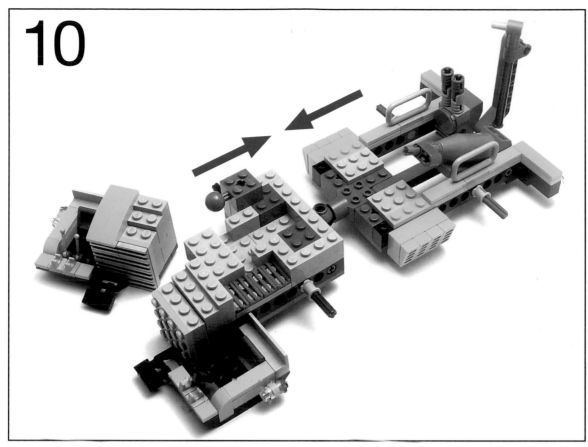

11

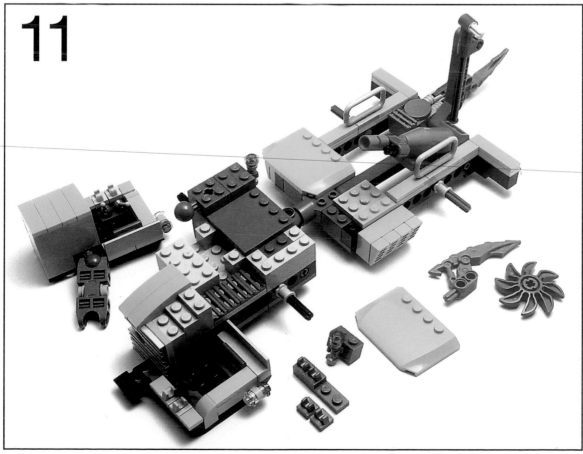

12

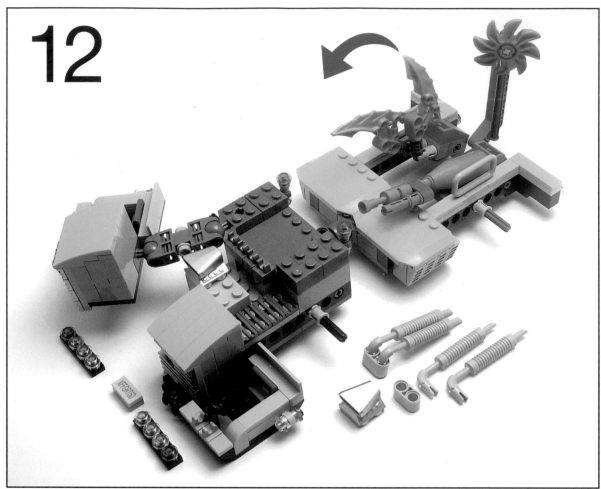

ANY WHEELS WITH A DIAMETER SIMILAR TO THESE WILL FIT ON THIS VEHICLE.

THE JACKKNIFE IS LOADED
WITH FUNCTIONS FOR
CRUSHING, CUTTING,
SCRAPING, AND MELTING
ROCKS—A VERY HANDY
PIECE OF EQUIPMENT
FOR US MINERS.

WOW, THAT JACKKNIFE IS A TOUGH BUILD, BUT WHAT A GREAT VEHICLE. THANKS!

NO PROBLEM, MEGS. HERE ARE SOME OF OUR OTHER MACHINES. FEEL FREE TO COPY ANY OF THEM SHOULD YOU NEED SOME HEAVY MACHINERY.

BUILDING JOURNAL

Looking at Moritz's mining equipment, I can see that all of the machines have some key details in common: protective roll cages, big industrial-looking engines, lots of lights, and, of course, bright colors. Bright colors make these big, dangerous vehicles easy to see. I should remember these details when I'm building heavy equipment.

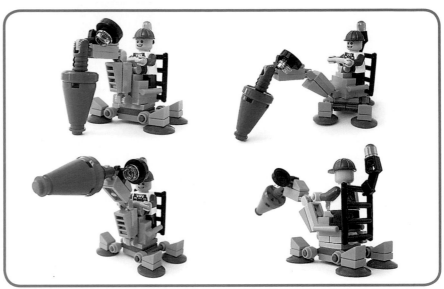

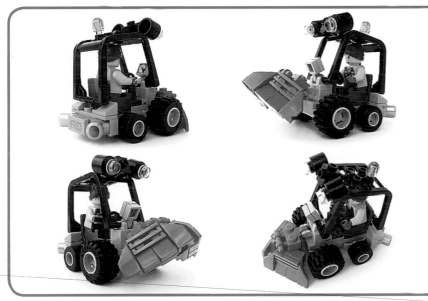

HERE IS WHERE WE HOUSE THE CAPTURED ROCK MONSTERS.

AWW, IT LOOKS THEY HAVE EVERYTHING THEY NEED: FOOD, WATER, AND A NICE HOUSE, TOO.

HEHE. YES, THE PROBLEM IS THEY GET IN OUR WAY ALL THE TIME! THIS GREEN GUY IS BRUTUS. HE IS A ROCK DRAGON, AND HE HELPS US KEEP THE WILD ROCK MONSTERS IN LINE. AS LONG AS WE GIVE HIM A FEW CRYSTALS, BRUTUS IS HAPPY.

BUILDING JOURNAL

Moritz showed me how a few slopes and some basic LEGO bricks can make a nice little house for a pet.

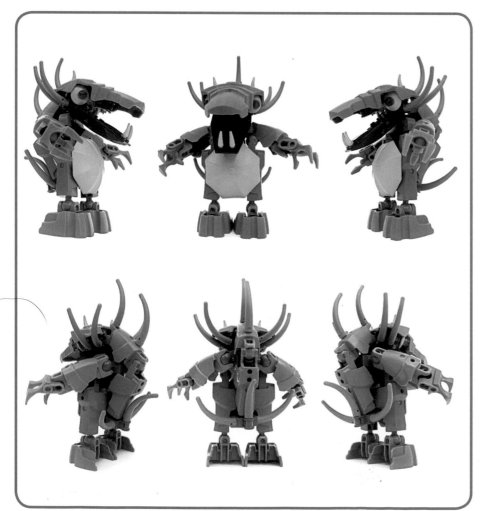

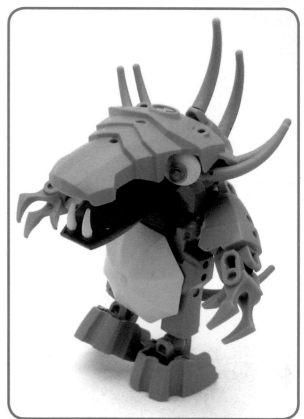

WOW, BRUTUS IS AWESOME!

UH-OH, MORE ROCK MONSTERS ON THE LOOSE! STOP EATING ALL OUR CRYSTALS!

MINE!!!

OH NO! BRUTUS IS ON AN ENERGY CRYSTAL RAMPAGE! TIME TO GO, MEGS!

YIKES! I'M OUTTA HERE, MORITZ!

Skywolf

The Sky's the Limit

Jon Hall

Nickname: jonhall18

Profession: Graphic Designer

Nationality: British

Website: *www.flickr.com/photos/25163007@N07/*

Gryphon

Scarlet Fury

Viper

Skyhammer

Steel Wind

The Phoenix

HERE'S ONE OF MY PLANES: THE *PHOENIX*. I CAN SHOW YOU HOW TO BUILD IT, BUT WATCH OUT— IT'S TRICKY! LET'S START WITH THE COCKPIT.

1

2

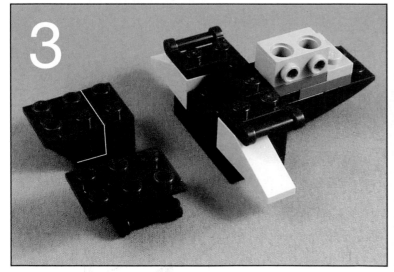

3

4

5

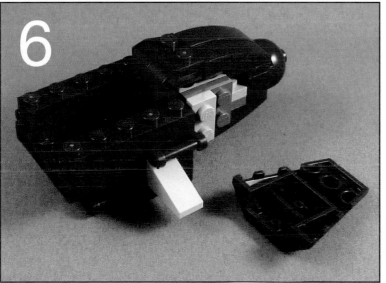

6

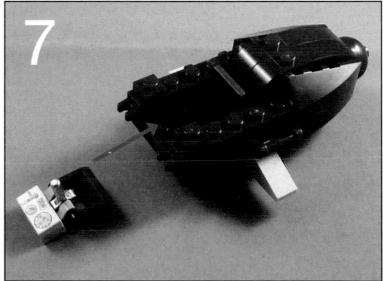

7

8

Building Tip
Make sure that your minifigure can fit into the cockpit before you build too much of your plane!

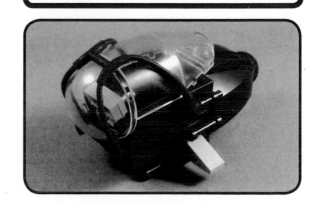

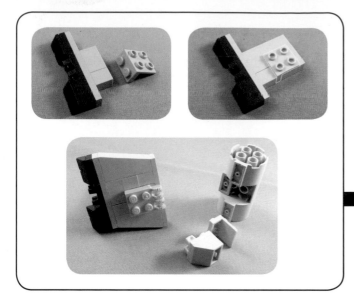

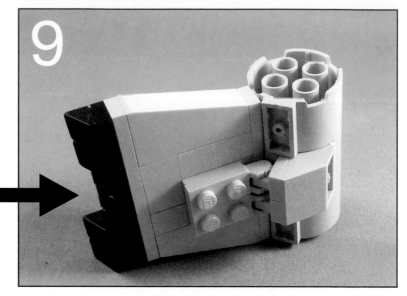

9

10

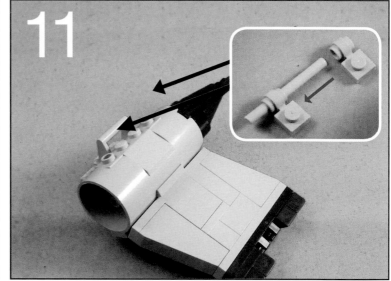

11

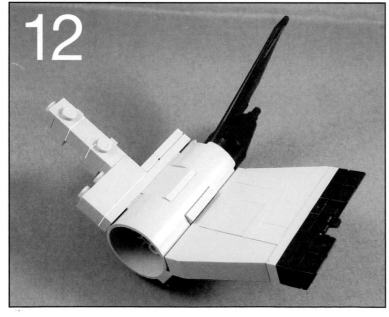

12

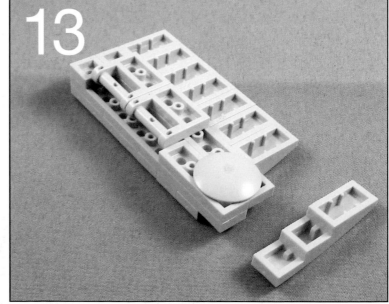

13

14

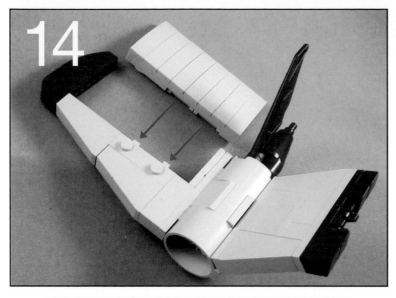

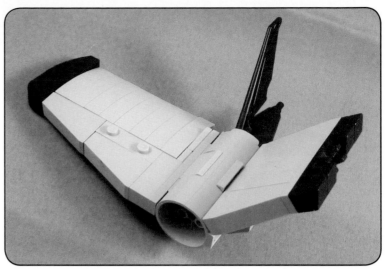

15

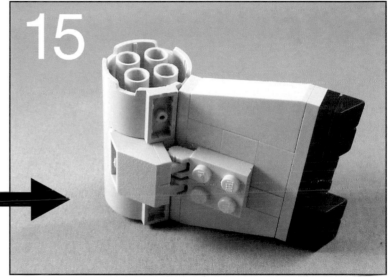

16

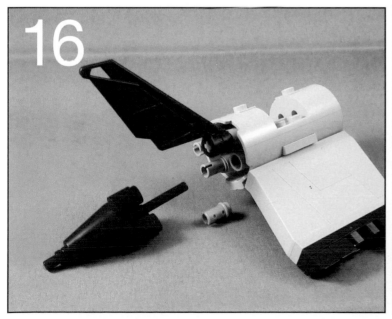

17

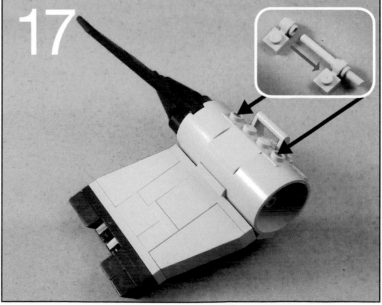

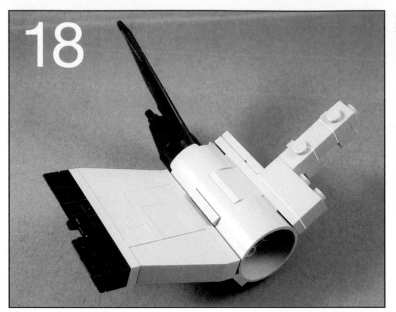

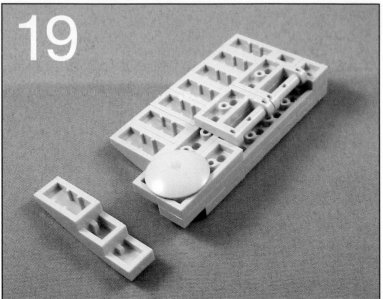

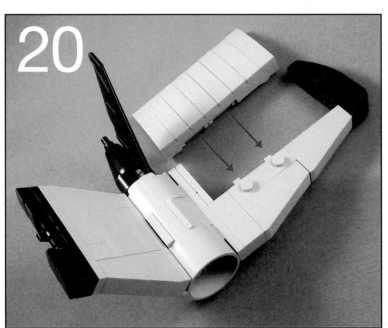

BUILDING JOURNAL

Jon's planes take advantage of the many curved and circular LEGO pieces. He has a talent for using elements so they flow from one into the next as if they belong together. This is something I should look at more closely in my own building. What slopes and curves can I use to smoothly form a cohesive shape? There must be millions of combinations.

21

22

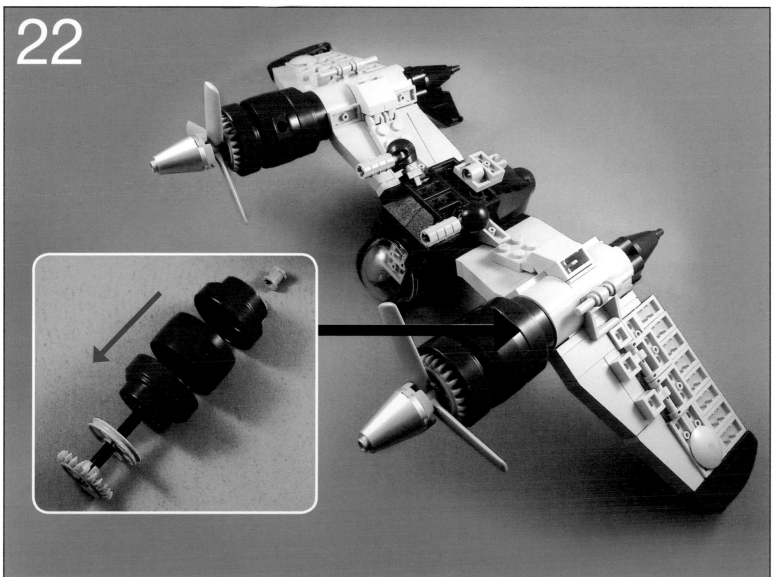

×2

BUILDING JOURNAL

Jon says: "Vehicles with interesting paint jobs often have sections that are painted bright colors and sections that aren't. You can re-create this effect by using differently colored bricks in different parts of your model."

THE *PHOENIX* IS A REAL BEAUTY. I BET SHE GOES REALLY FAST!

WELL, I'M NOT EXACTLY SURE, BUT IT MUST BE PRETTY FAST SINCE I CAN BEAM IN AND OUT OF WORLDS INSTANTANEOUSLY. BRICKBOT, CLOCK MY SPEED! SEE YOU LATER, JON!

THANKS! SHE IS PRETTY FAST. HOW ABOUT YOUR RIDE?

The Turtle Factory

Pete Reid

Nickname: Legoloverman

Profession: Author

Nationality: British

Website: *www.flickr.com/photos/legoloverman/*

BUILDING JOURNAL

Pete told me it can take a long time to build a cool LEGO robot. I should gather my smallest pieces and consider the best combinations.

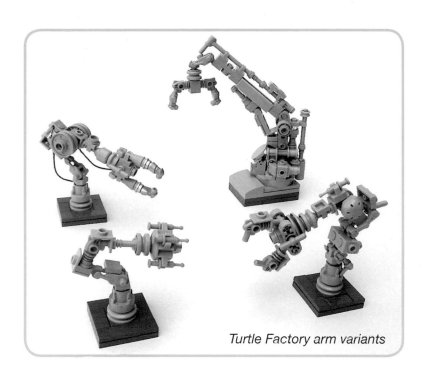

Turtle Factory arm variants

YOU DON'T NEED A FACTORY TO BUILD YOUR OWN SPACE TURTLE-BOT. TRY BUILDING THEM IN DIFFERENT COLORS, AND USE OTHER LEGO PIECES TO MAKE DIFFERENT LEGS AND GUNS. GO ON, HAVE A GO!

Space Turtles

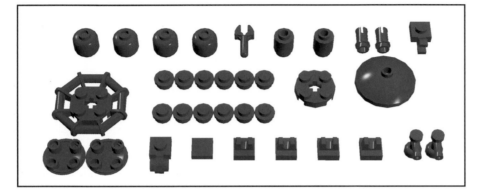

1

2

3

4 ×4

5

6

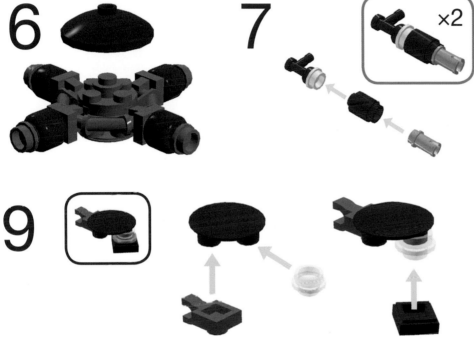

7

×2

8

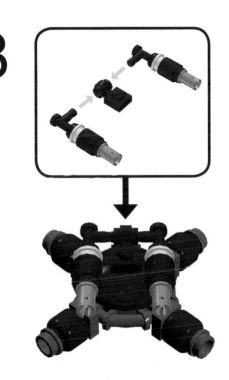

9

10

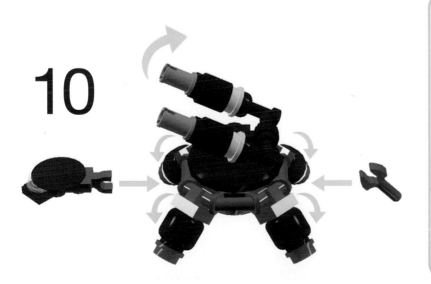

Peter Morris

Nickname: peterlmorris, aka Rival M

Profession: Stay-at-Home Dad

Nationality: American

Website: *www.flickr.com/photos/rival_m/*

OKAY, GET READY TO BUILD MY STARFIGHTER! PAY CLOSE ATTENTION. YOU'LL HAVE TO STUDY MY BREAKDOWN CLOSELY.

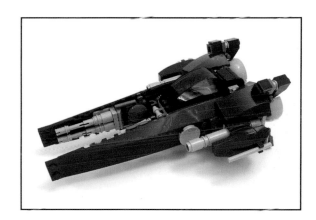

Seraph Starfighter

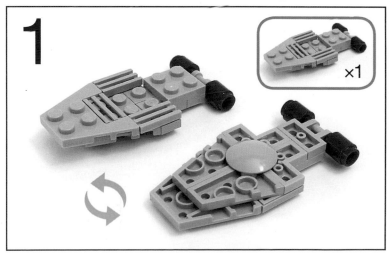

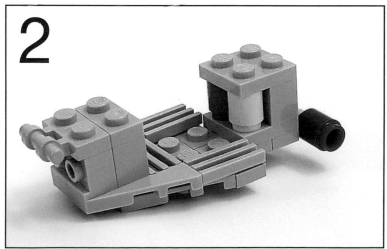

3

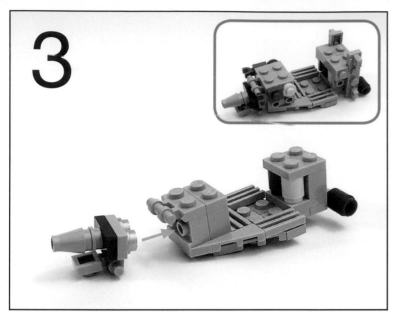

4

Building Tip
The far side of the model is a perfect mirror to the side you can see here.

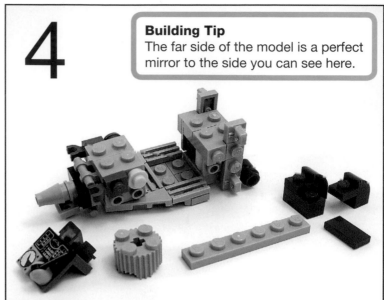

5

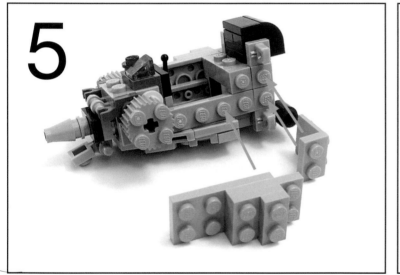

6

×2

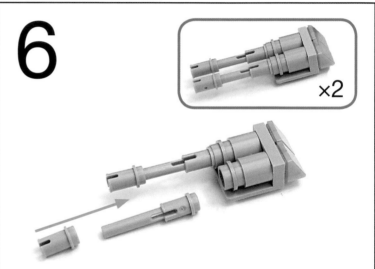

7

×2

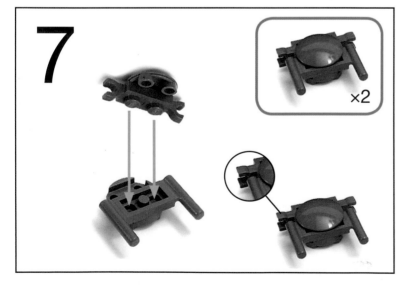

8

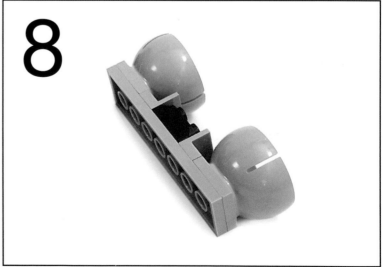

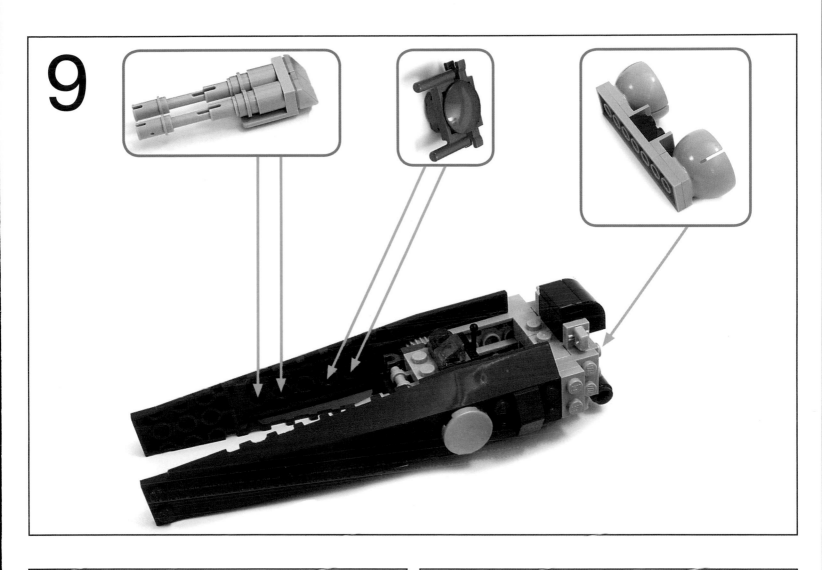

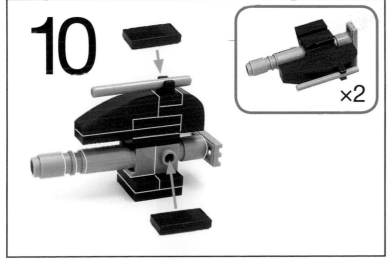

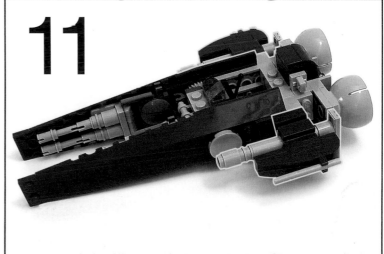

12

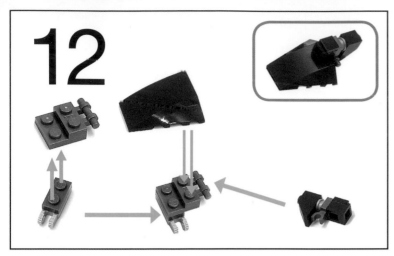

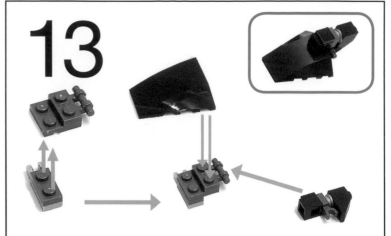

13

14

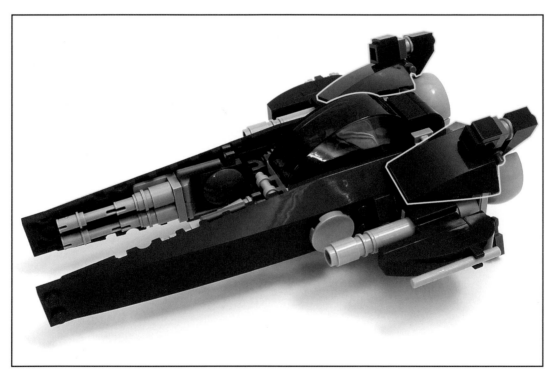

15

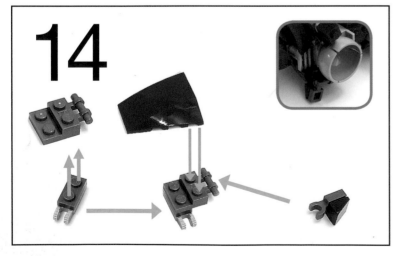

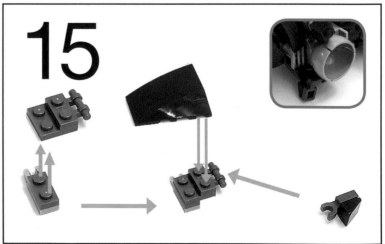

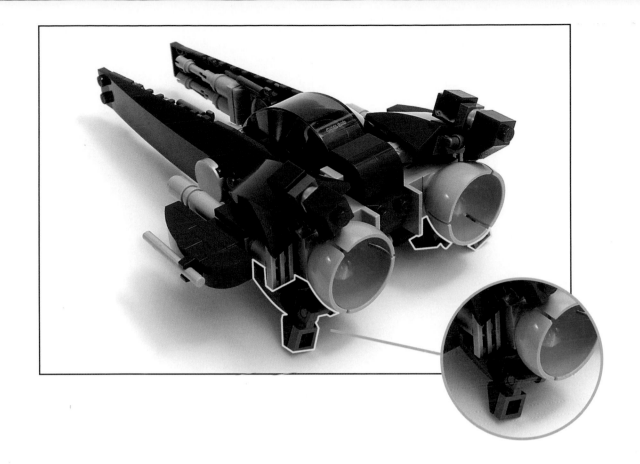

WHY DO YOU USE SO MANY OF THESE BRACKETS? SO YOU CAN BUILD SIDEWAYS?

YES, USING THEM I'VE CREATED A SIMPLE WAY TO BUILD DIFFERENTLY CONFIGURED STARFIGHTERS QUICKLY. I HAVE A LOT OF SKETCHES AND IDEAS FOR SHIPS, BUT IF I BUILT A SEPARATE COCKPIT FOR EACH ONE I'D NEVER FINISH! SO I HAVE DESIGNED A SERIES OF SIMPLE COCKPIT BOXES THAT ALLOW FOR LOTS OF VARIATIONS. HERE, CHECK OUT THESE COCKPIT SCHEMATICS.

Cockpits

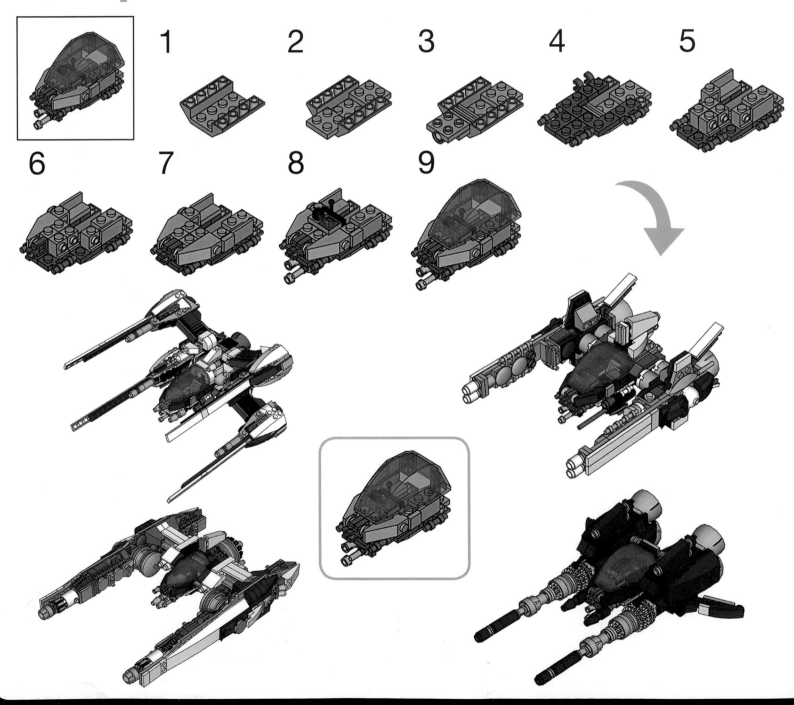

1

2

3

4

5

6

7

8

9

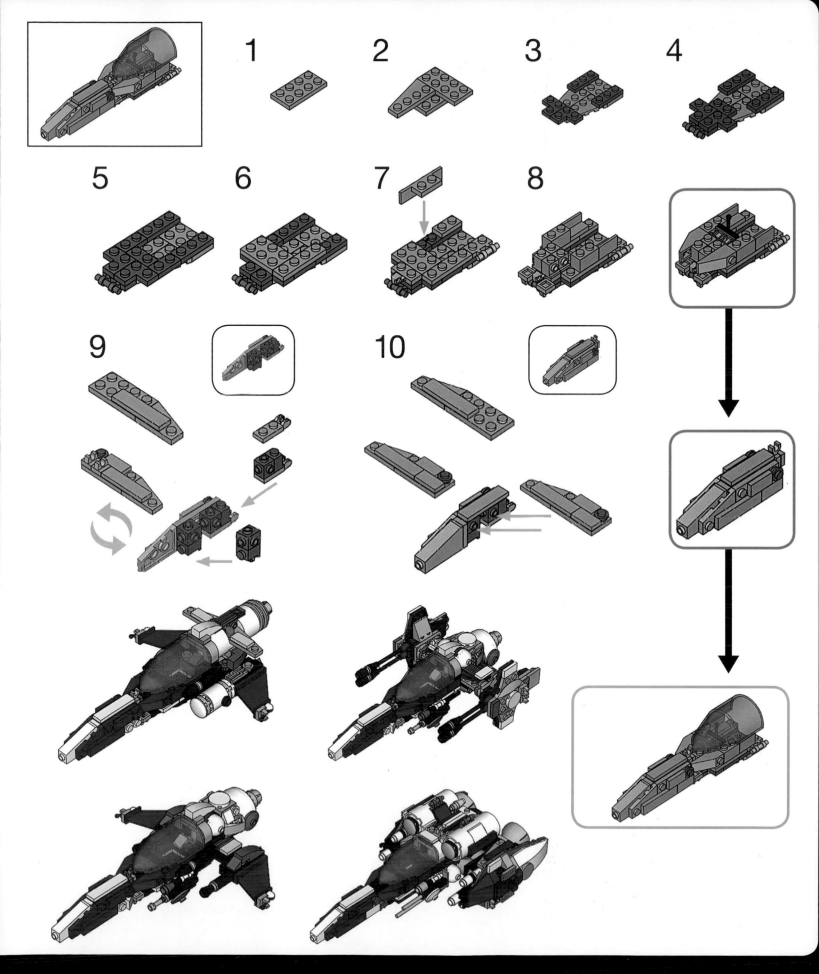

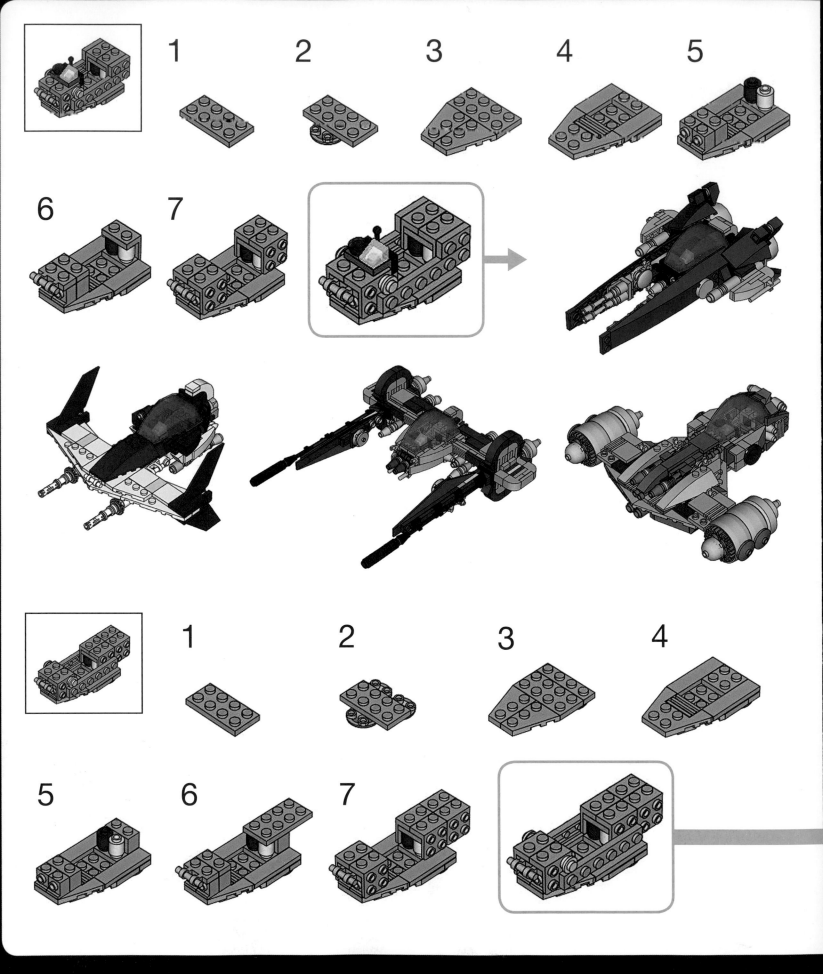

1

2

3

4

5

6

7

1

2

3

4

5

6

7

THESE COCKPIT INSTRUCTIONS ARE A STARTING POINT. EACH STARFIGHTER HAS SLIGHT VARIATIONS, AND THE BOXES JUST PROVIDE A FOUNDATION. THE POSSIBILITIES ARE ENDLESS. JUST REMEMBER, WHEN YOU ARE DESIGNING YOUR COCKPIT BE SURE TO LEAVE ROOM FOR A PILOT!

WHERE DO YOU GET THE INSPIRATION FOR YOUR FIGHTERS?

SOMETIMES I START WITH A PENCIL SKETCH; OTHER TIMES I'M INSPIRED BY SOMEONE ELSE'S LEGO MODEL OR SOME CONCEPT ART. AND SOMETIMES I JUST BUILD WITH LEGO PIECES THAT I THINK LOOK COOL.

WHAT HAPPENS WHEN YOU'RE STUMPED? DO YOU EVER GET FRUSTRATED WITH A BUILD?

ABSOLUTELY. SOMETIMES I JUST PUT AN UNFINISHED BUILD IN A DRAWER AND COME BACK TO IT LATER, BUT I NEVER GIVE UP. IF I CAN IMAGINE IT, I CAN USUALLY BUILD IT. IT'S LEGO BRICKS THAT MAKE THAT POSSIBLE!

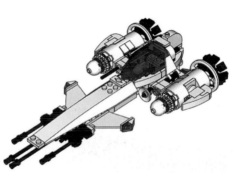

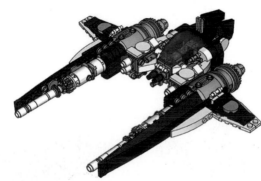

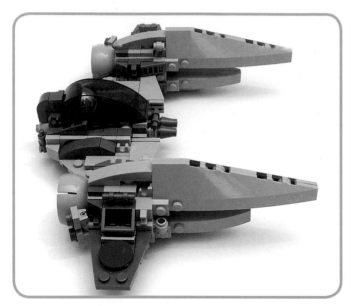

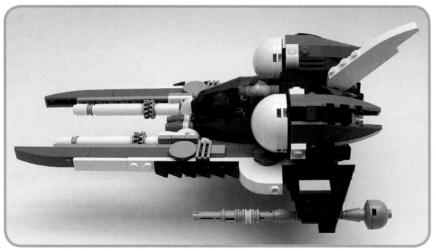

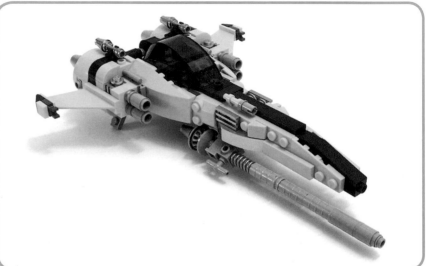

THESE ARE EPIC SHIPS! THEY GIVE ME LOTS OF IDEAS!

THANKS! IF YOU'RE LOOKING FOR MORE SCI-FI IDEAS, YOU SHOULD TRY VISITING MARK. HE'S EASY TO FIND: JUST HEAD EAST FROM HERE AND FOLLOW THE SOUND OF BIG GUNS AND PLASTIC BRICKS!

THANKS FOR EVERYTHING, PETER.

NO PROBLEM, MEGS. I'M ALWAYS HAPPY TO GIVE BUILDING ADVICE.

Mighty Mecha

Mark Stafford

Nickname: Nabii

Profession: Designer

Nationality: British

Website: *www.flickr.com/photos/nabii*

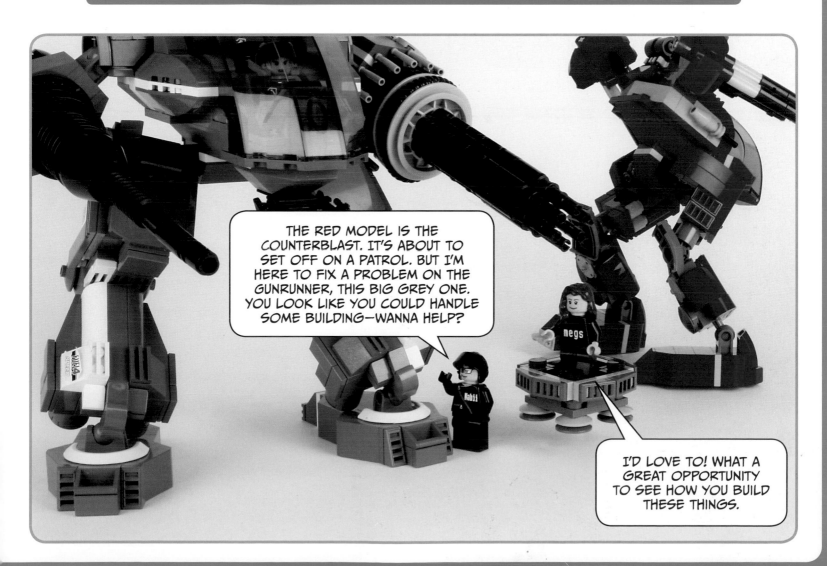

SEE THE PROBLEM HERE? THE ARM IS ALL FLOPPY. I MADE A BASIC BUILDING ERROR WHEN I FIRST BUILT IT.

YES?

I CHOSE THE WRONG HINGE FOR THE SHOULDER. NORMALLY A BALL JOINT LIKE THIS WOULD HOLD THE WEIGHT OF AN ARM, BUT THIS MECHA HAS REALLY HEAVY ARMS. I SHOULD HAVE USED ONE OF THESE CLICK HINGE BALL JOINTS INSTEAD.

SO WE JUST SWAP OUT THAT HINGE FOR THIS ONE HERE?

THAT'S THE IDEA.

Counterblast

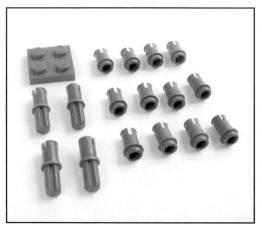

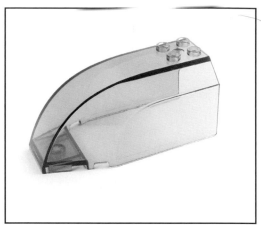

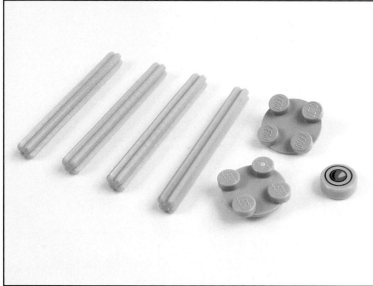

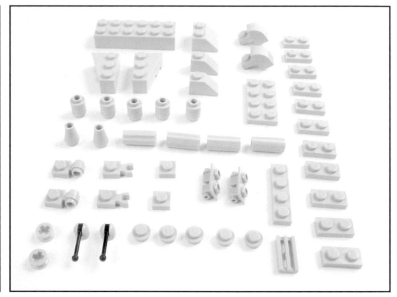

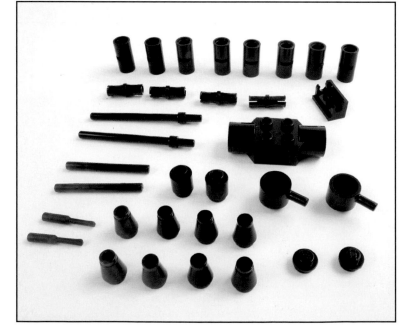

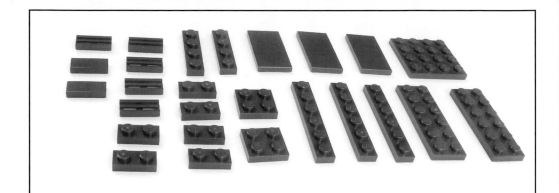

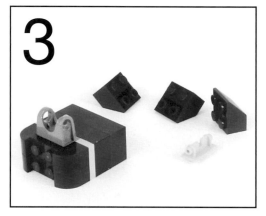

×2

1

2
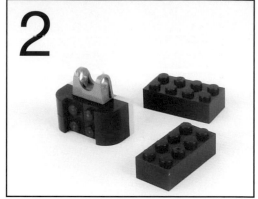

3
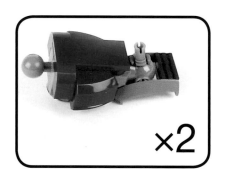

4

5

×2

6

7

8
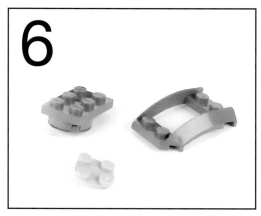

9

10
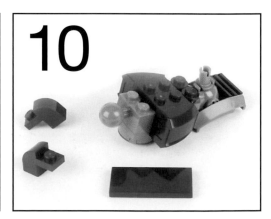

11

12

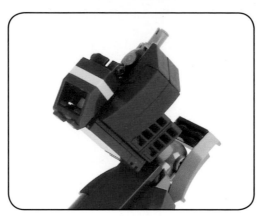

13

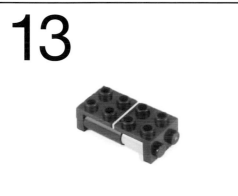

14

15

16

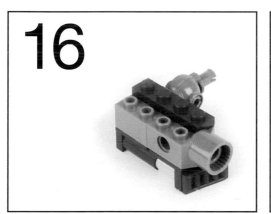

17

18

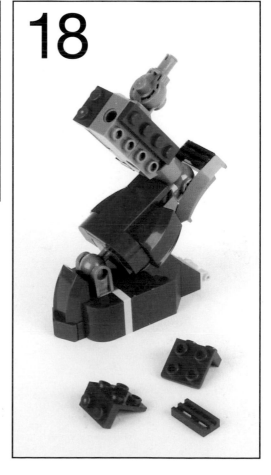

Building Tip
Building in a stop (a point beyond which the leg will not bend) will keep the legs of your mecha strong and increase stability.

19

20

21

NOW THAT YOU'VE BUILT THE LEFT LEG, YOU NEED TO MIRROR IT TO BUILD THE RIGHT LEG.

22

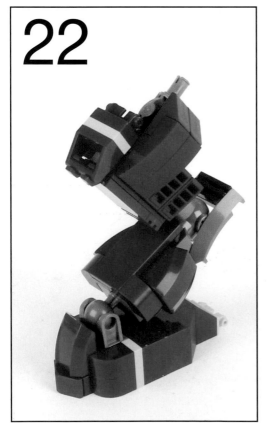

23

24

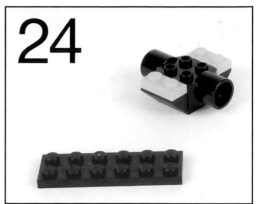

25

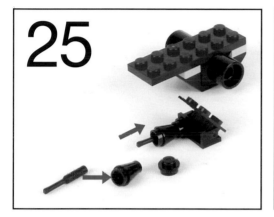

26

27

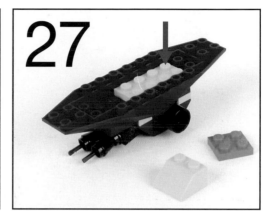

28

29

30

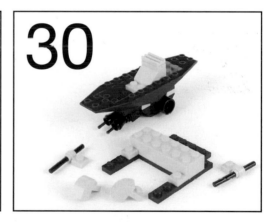

31

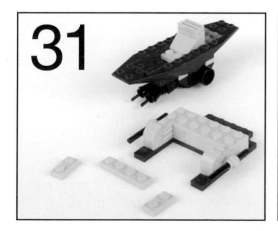

32

33

34

35

36

37

38

39

40

41

42

43

44

45

×2

46

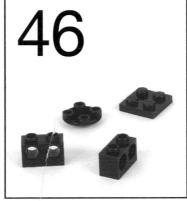

47

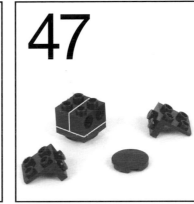

48

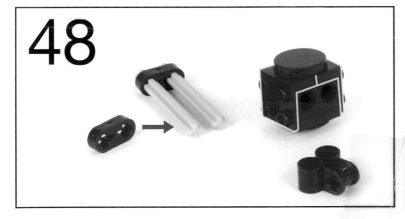

49

50

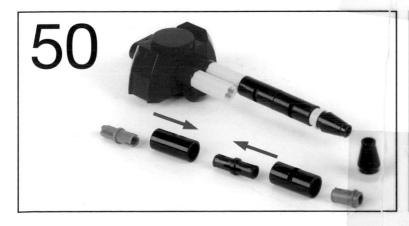

51

52

53

54

55

56

57

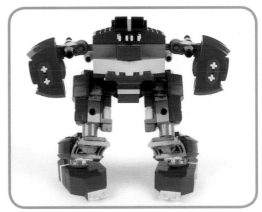

Building Tip
Of course, your mecha doesn't have to have two identical arms. How about adding a rocket pod or a power sword instead?

YEAH, THOSE ARE SOME COOL ALTERNATIVE ARMS!

Mecha Inspiration

BUILDING JOURNAL

Mark explained to me the frame of a mecha is the most important thing to figure out. You need to plan your mecha's proportions from the start. Does it have long legs or arms? Does the pilot sit in the body, or is there a head on top? Does it have two, four, or more arms and legs? Do the knees bend backwards (like in the Counterblast), or do they work more like a human's?

Only once you've built a basic frame is it time to decide on other key apsects, like whether it will be heavily armored and slow or lightly armored and fleet footed. But mecha aren't all military. They can be walking forklifts, farming mecha, or even racing mechs. I wonder what my Transport-o-lux would look like with legs?

Building Tip
Try finding LEGO parts that fit with the theme of your mecha. These small details add a lot of character to your model.

Building Tip
You can break up color schemes by adding accent colors. Try creating stripes or blocks of color.

THIS GREY COUNTERBLAST WAS THE FIRST ONE I BUILT. I THINK THE DESIGN IS STRONG ENOUGH TO BUILD IN WHICHEVER LEGO BRICK COLORS YOU HAVE.

DEFINITELY! THANKS FOR SHOWING ME HOW YOU BUILD MECHA, MARK.

MY PLEASURE!

Megs, I've been tinkering with your space-time controls. I think I can beam you to a builder in another time period.

REALLY, BRICKBOT? LET'S DO IT!

TAKE CARE, MEGS. COME BACK SOMETIME, AND I'LL SHOW YOU SOME OF MY STARSHIPS!

I WILL. PROMISE.

Merchant Wagon

Medieval Village

Aaron Andrews

Nickname: DARKspawn

Profession: Music Teacher

Nationality: Australian

Websites: *www.flickr.com/photos/darkspawn/*
www.brickshelf.com/cgi-bin/gallery.cgi?m=DARKspawn

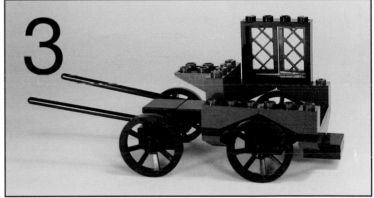

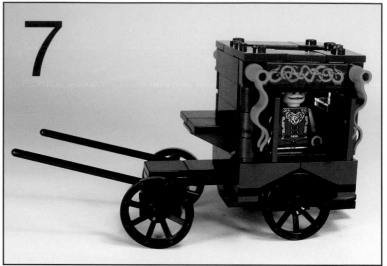

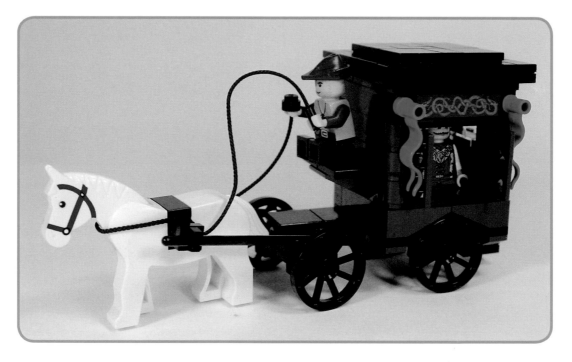

NOW LET'S BUILD A BUTCHER SHOP. FIRST, CREATE SOME LAND BY STACKING LEGO PLATES ON TOP OF ONE ANOTHER.

Butcher Shop

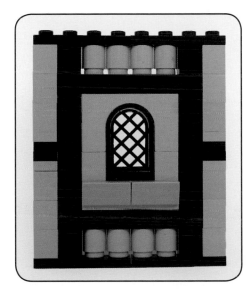

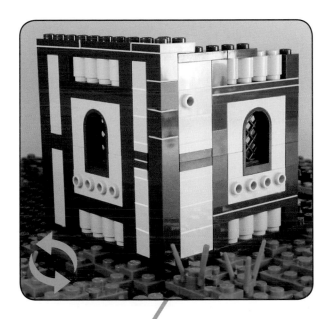

1

2

3

4

5

Building Tip
Place a 1×6 black plate underneath the roof so it does not slide off.

6

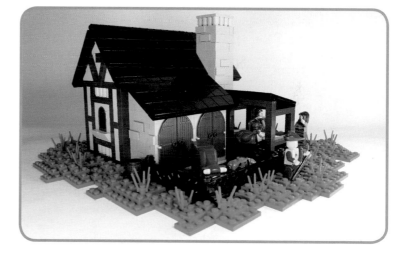

BUILDING JOURNAL

Texture is very important for adding detail to your models. There are several LEGO bricks with patterns in them, and you can use these to give your models a more realistic look. Aaron has also added interest to his stone walls by placing tiles sideways so they look like bricks sticking out of the stonework. He has also laid out the tiles on the roof to look like square slates, just like on a real old building!

Harold's House

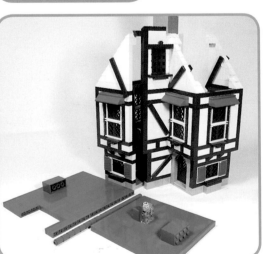

Hilltop Tower

THIS YELLOW TOWER REMINDS ME OF SOMETHING FROM WHEN I WAS YOUNGER...

YES, IT'S A TRIBUTE TO THE FIRST EVER LEGO CASTLE MODEL: THE *CLASSIC YELLOW CASTLE*. I HAD IT AS A CHILD.

OH, YES! ME TOO!

IF YOU EVER MEET THE ORIGINAL DESIGNER ON YOUR TRAVELS, TELL HIM HOW MANY OF US HE INSPIRED!

BUILDING JOURNAL

I noticed in Aaron's medieval models that the LEGO black and brown colors both represent wood. This technique adds visual detail simply by using color. If he had used just brown or just black, his models would have been very bland. In his market model, for example, I can see how he separates the browns of the ground from the browns of the wooden beams in the town well by using light grey "stone" tiles to break things up.

Medieval Market

Woodsman's Cottage

HERE IS A SIMPLE WOODSMAN'S COTTAGE. ADDING SMALL OUTBUILDINGS HELPS GROW YOUR MEDIEVAL VILLAGE.

REMEMBER WHEN BUILDING IN THE MIDDLE AGES THEME TO SHOW ANIMALS, FLAGS, FENCES, TREES, AND OTHER DETAIL ELEMENTS TO MAKE YOUR MODELS LOOK MORE AUTHENTIC.

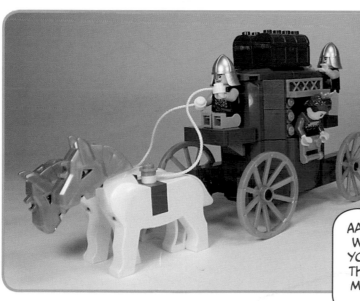

AARON, IT LOOKS AMAZING WHEN YOU BRING ALL OF YOUR MODELS TOGETHER. THANK YOU FOR SHOWING ME HOW YOU BUILD YOUR MEDIEVAL MODELS.

IT WAS FUN, MEGS. WHERE ARE YOU HEADING NOW?

FURTHER BACK IN TIME, I THINK. BYE, AARON!

FARE THEE WELL, FAIR MAIDEN!

Triassic Park

Mike Psiaki

Nickname: Psiaki

Profession: Mechanical Engineer

Nationality: American

Website: *www.flickr.com/photos/pmiaki*

I BET THEY CAN RUN QUITE FAST. MAYBE YOU SHOULD BUILD A VEHICLE TO KEEP UP WITH THEM.

GREAT IDEA. LET'S BUILD A SAFARI TRUCK!

Building Tip
Both sides of the truck are symmetrical, so think carefully about how the model is built. Study the parts you can see to figure out the parts you can't see.

Safari Truck

1

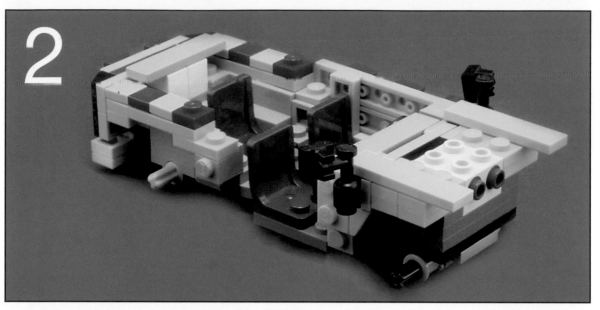

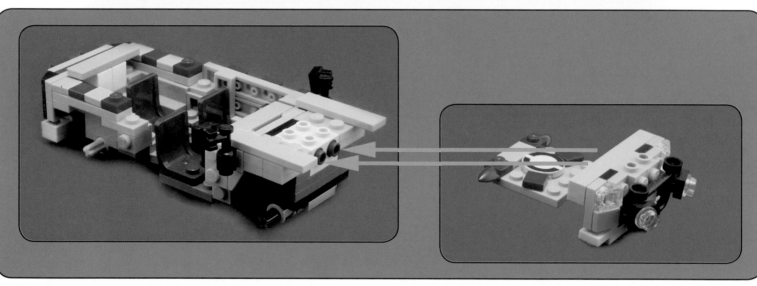

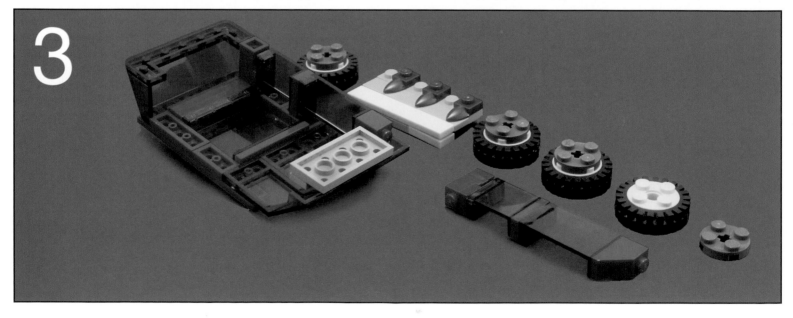

Pterosaur

Stegosaurus

THE STEGOSAURUS IS A MORE COMPLICATED BUILD. LET'S START WITH HIS HEAD.

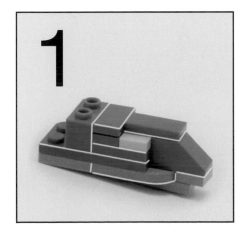
1

2

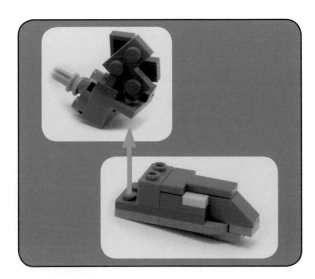

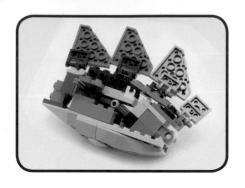

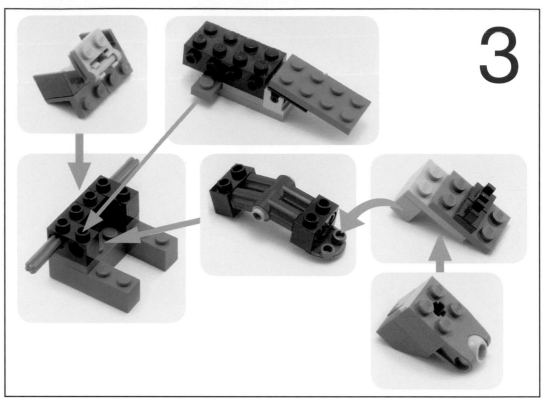

3

4

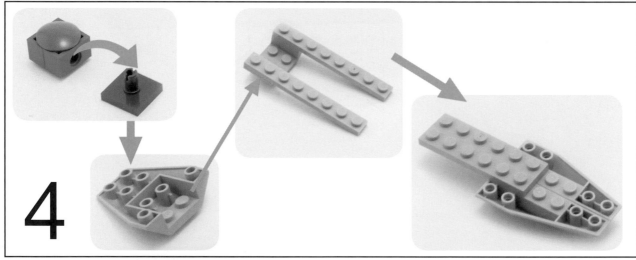

5

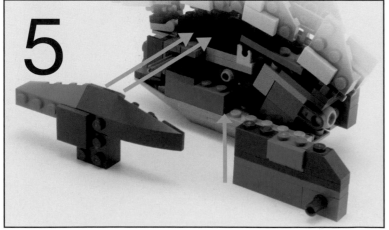

6

7

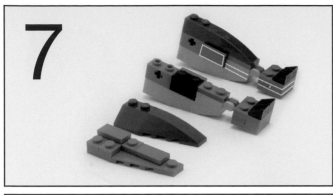

8

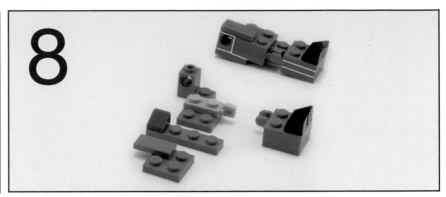

9

10

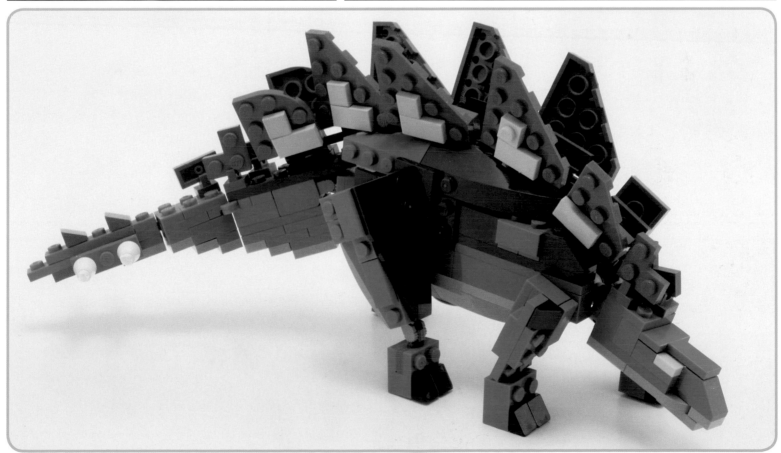

T. Rex

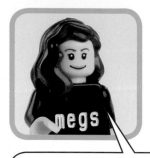

AWESOME STEGO. ANY CHANCE YOU CAN SHOW ME HOW TO BUILD THAT T. REX?

FOR AN EXPERIENCED BUILDER LIKE YOU, MEGS, OF COURSE. THIS IS A CHALLENGING BUILD!

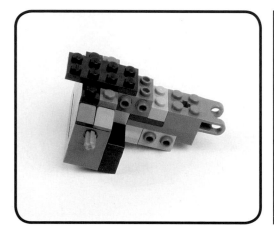

1

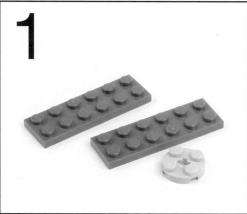

2

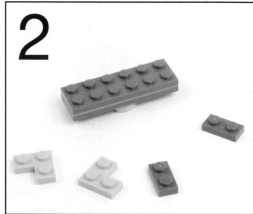

3

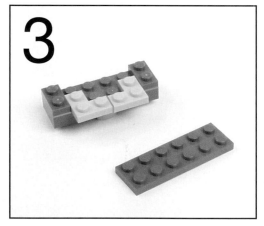

4

5

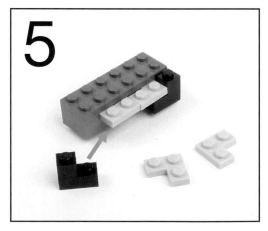

6

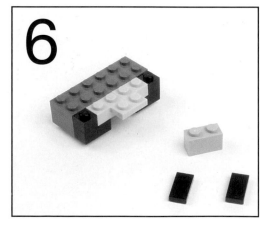

7

8

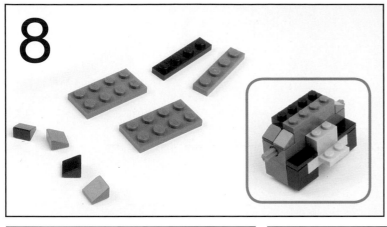

9

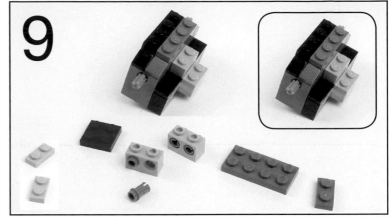

10

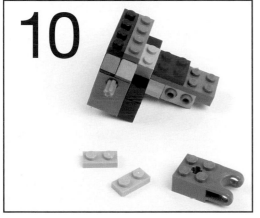

11

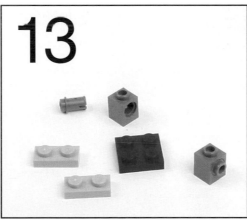

12

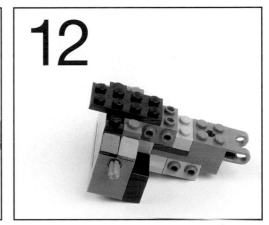

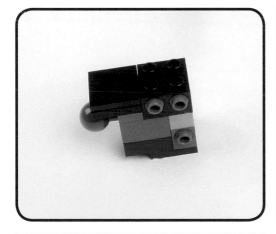

13

14

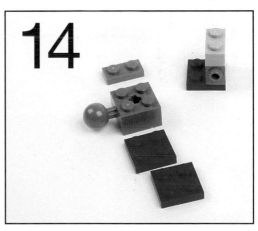

15

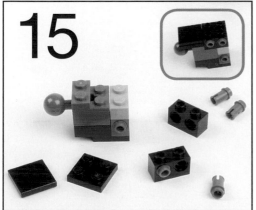

16

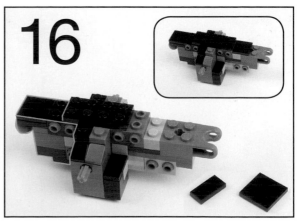

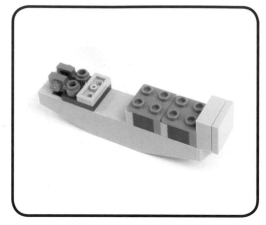

17

18

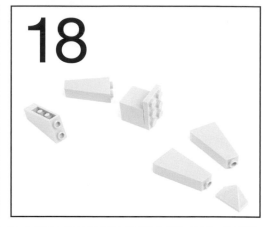

19

20

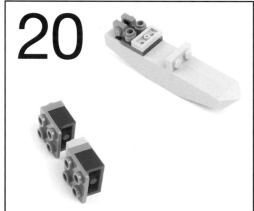

21

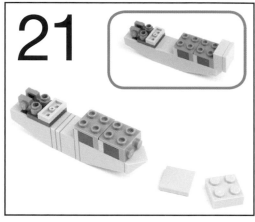

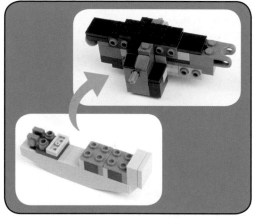

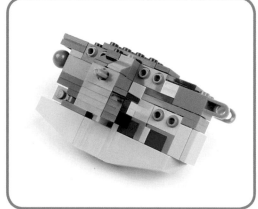

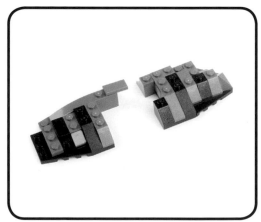

22

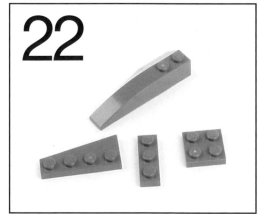

23

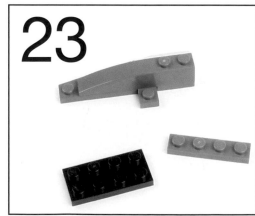

24

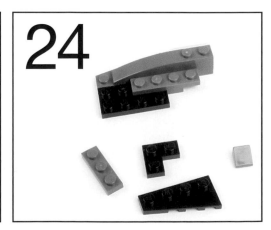

25

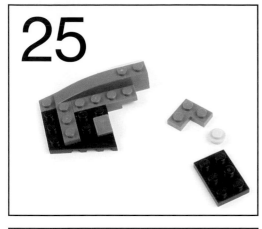

26

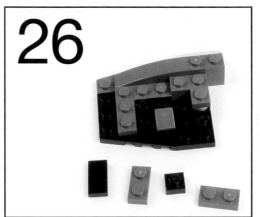

27

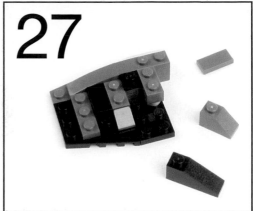

28

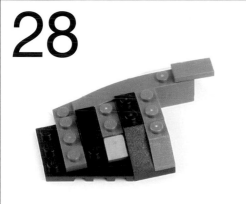

29

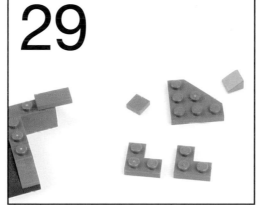

30

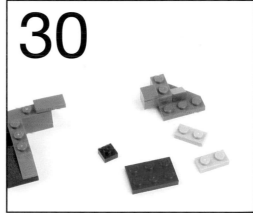

31

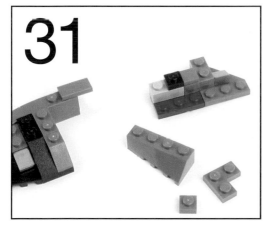

32

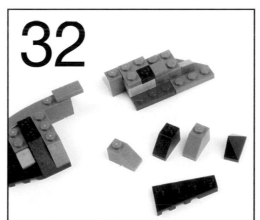

33

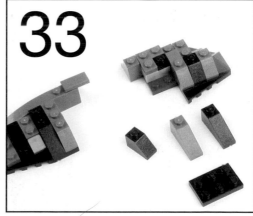

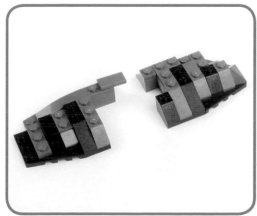

34

35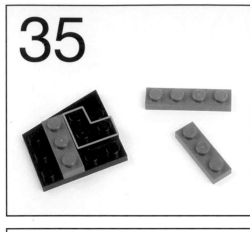

36

37

38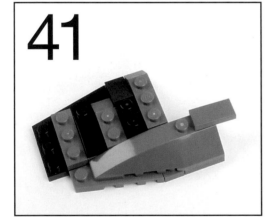

39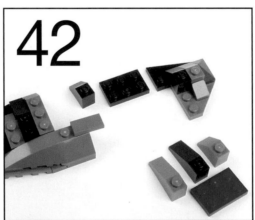

40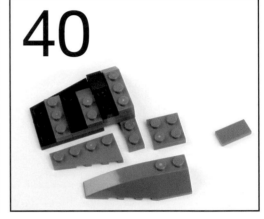

41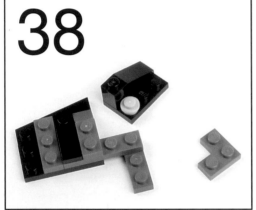

42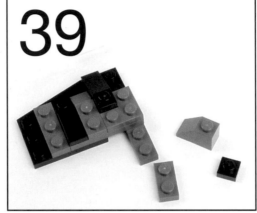

43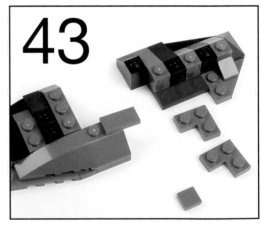

44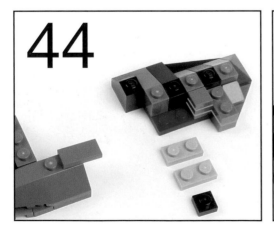

45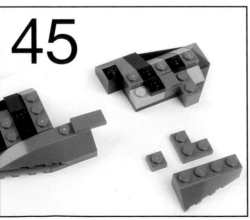

46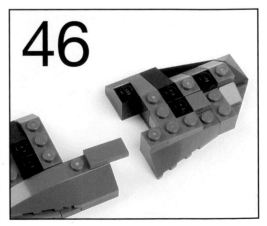

47

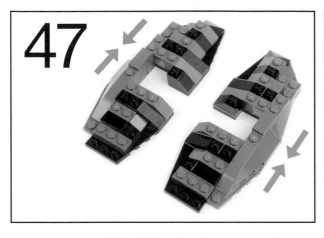

48

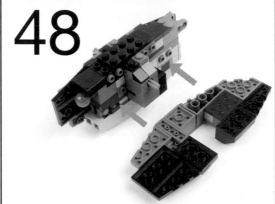

49

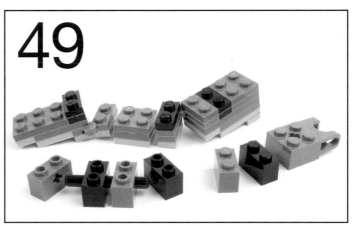

50

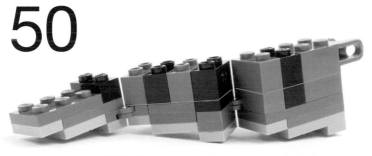

51

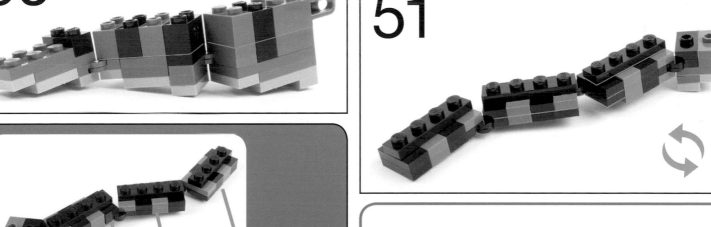

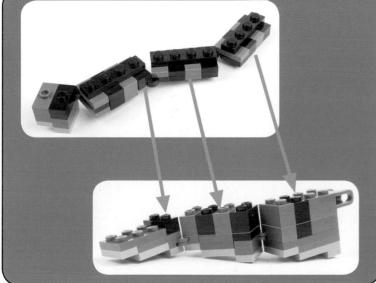

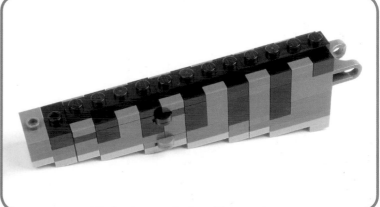

52

 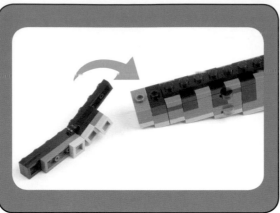 

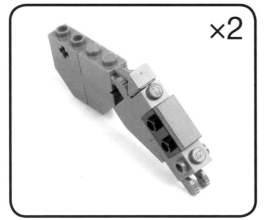
×2

53

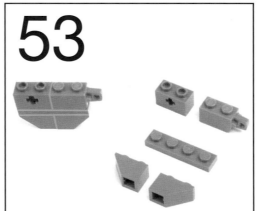

54

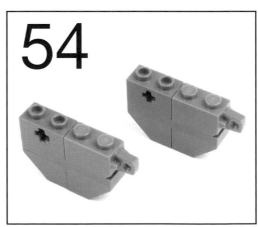

55

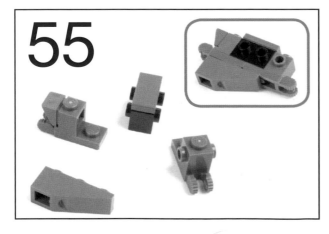

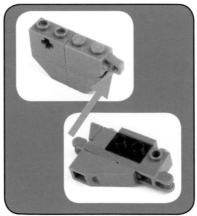

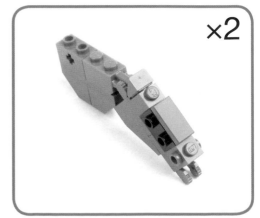
×2

56

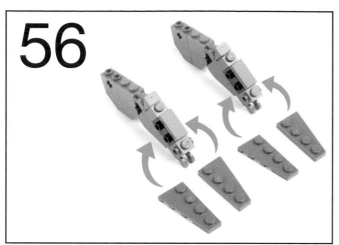

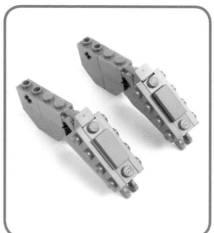

57

58

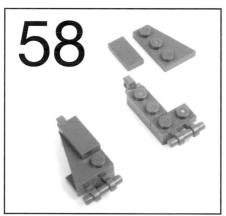

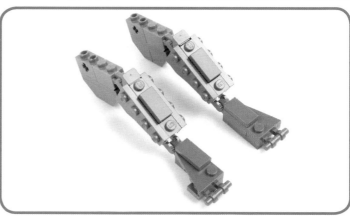

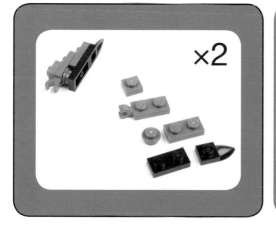

×2

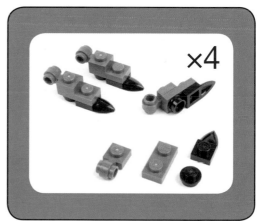

×4

59

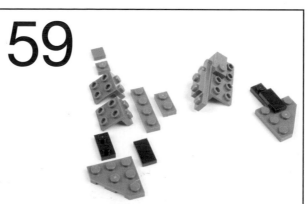

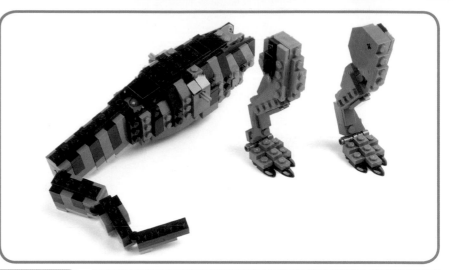

60

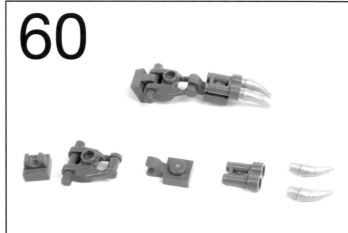

61

62

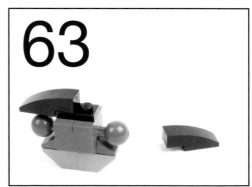

63

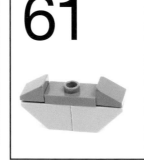

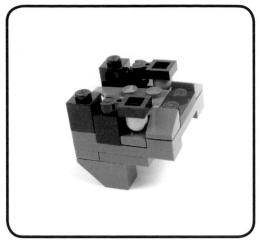

64

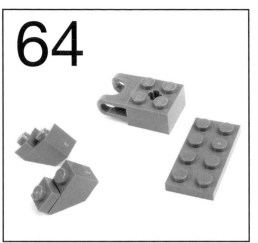

65

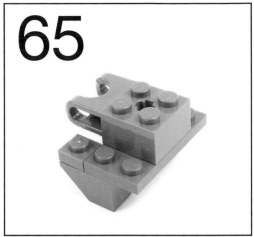

66

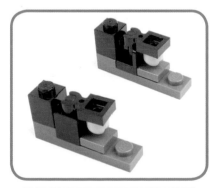

67

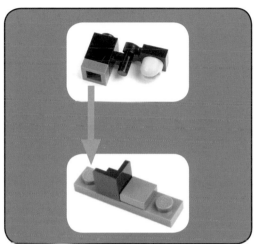

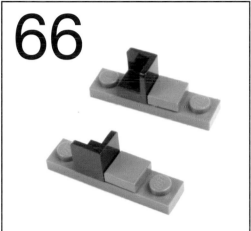

68

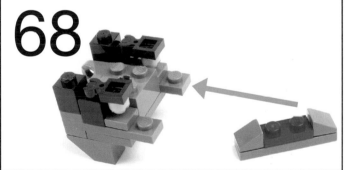

69

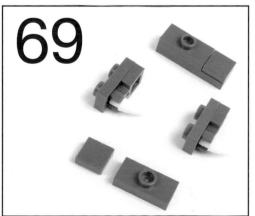

70

71

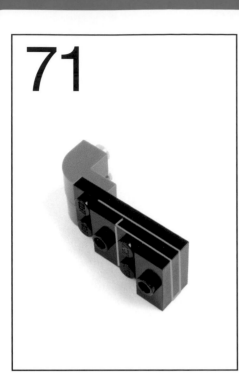

72

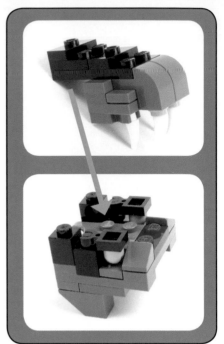

73

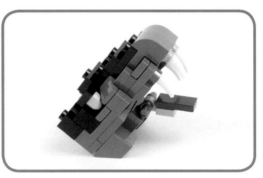

74

75

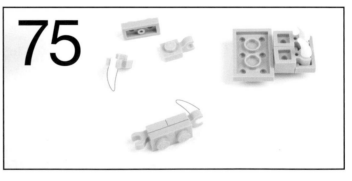

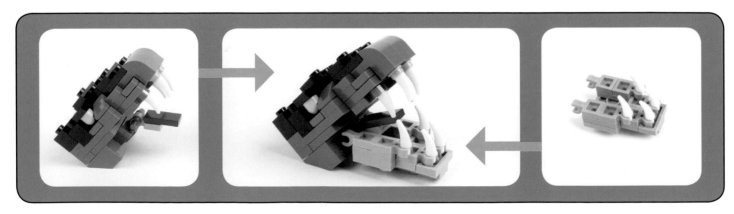

THAT WAS A LONG BUILD BUT TOTALLY WORTH IT!

THANKS! I HAVE ONE IN BROWN, TOO. SOMETIMES IT'S FUN TO BUILD A COPY OF A LEGO MODEL WITH A DIFFERENT COLOR SCHEME.

IF YOU WOULD LIKE A *BIG* CHALLENGE, YOU CAN ALWAYS TRY TO BUILD MY BRACHIOSAURUS.

DANG! HE SURE IS TALL! I'M NOT SURE I HAVE ENOUGH GREY LEGO BRICKS TO BUILD HIM, BUT I COULD TRY A BLUE ONE! HEEHEE.

THANK YOU, MIKE. I'M GOING TO CONTINUE MY EXPLORATION NOW, SO I'LL SAY GOOD-BYE.

BYE, MEGS. GOOD LUCK OUT THERE!

RUH-ROOH?

ROOOAAARRRR!

OH NO, NOW THERE ARE TWO OF THEM! WHERE DID I PARK THAT TRUCK? *AHHH!!*

Making New Friends

Katie Walker

Nickname: Eilonwy77

Profession: Elementary School Teacher

Nationality: American

Website: *www.flickr.com/eilonwy77*

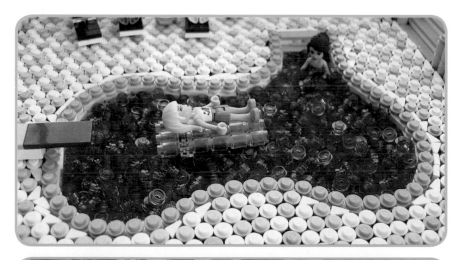

I'D LOVE TO SHARE MY TECHNIQUES! BUILDING A CURVED WALL STARTS WITH A SIMPLE BRICK SUBASSEMBLY.

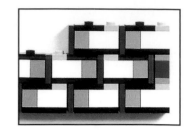

Curved Wall

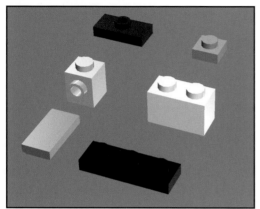

1

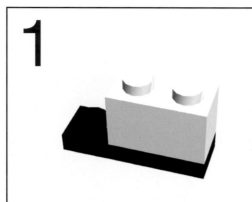

2

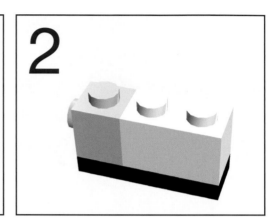

3

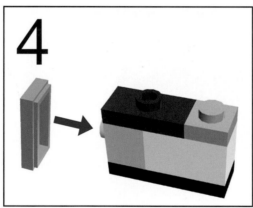

4

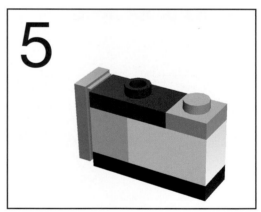

5

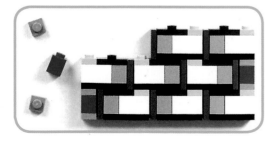

Building Tip
Switch directions with each layer to make your wall more stable.

NOW I'LL SHOW YOU HOW TO BUILD A MOSAIC THAT'S SIX STUDS WIDE AND NINE STUDS LONG. MOSAIC BUILDING IS A LITTLE UNUSUAL. WE'LL START BY BUILDING A FRAME TO HOLD THE PIECES. AFTER THAT, WE JUST SLOT IN SLOPE AND TILE PIECES SIDEWAYS. THE PATTERN WILL NEED TO FIT THE FRAME *EXACTLY*.

Mosaic

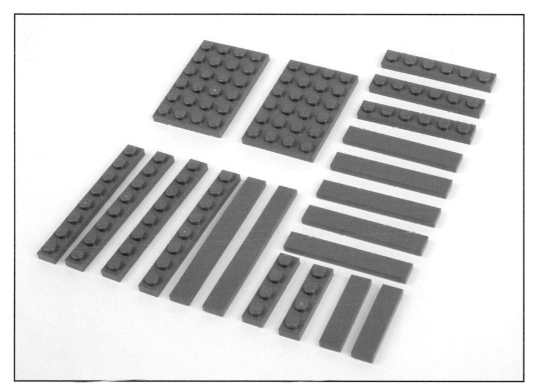

1
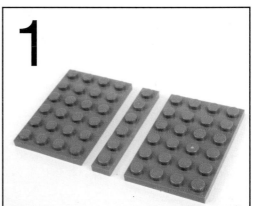

2
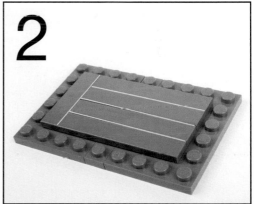

3
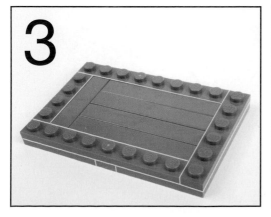

4
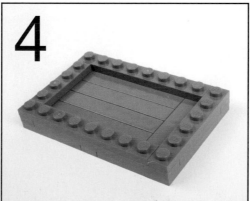

5
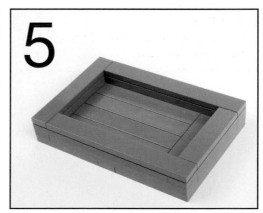

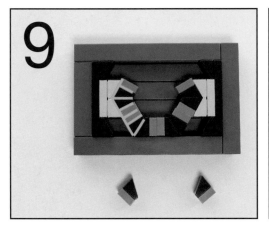

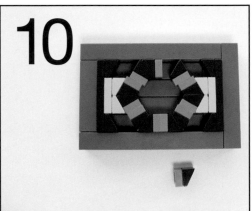

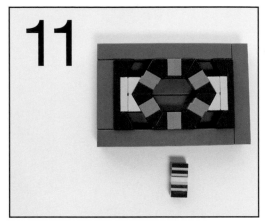

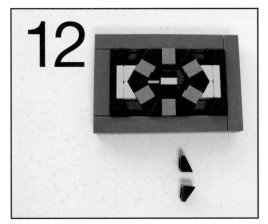

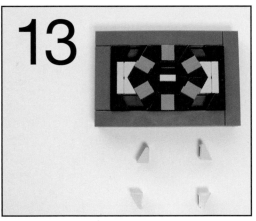

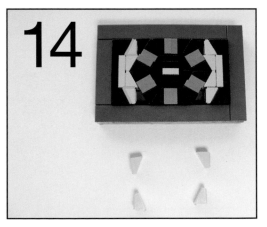

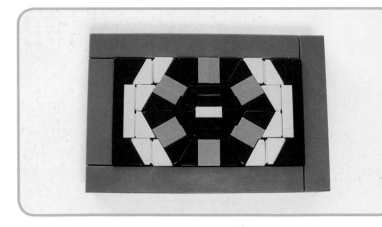

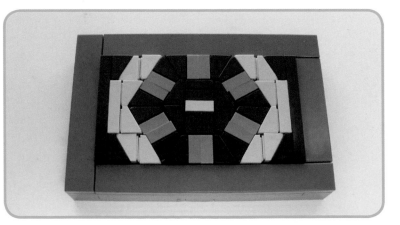

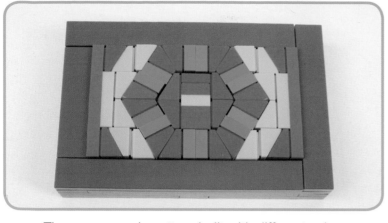

The same mosaic pattern built with different colors

THIS WOULD BE A NICE RUG FOR MY IDEA LAB.

Building Tip

This design is really tight, and you might think several pieces won't fit. The last piece of the hexagon is especially difficult to squeeze in. Try squeezing the smallest part of the piece into the gap first and then push hard. When you're finished, you might be able to hold the mosaic upside down without any of the pieces falling out.

This mosaic is designed with several pieces attached to each other, which makes them easier to place. Having fewer loose pieces also increases the tension that holds the mosaic in place and makes it less likely to fall apart.

YOU CAN ALSO BUILD A MOSAIC USING OTHER LEGO BRICKS, LIKE THIS PINK AND BLUE ONE.

Katie told me mosaics are really finicky. Sometimes just modifying the frame slightly will completely change how a mosaic fits into place. She recommends trying different ideas, no matter how crazy they seem. Even if the original idea doesn't work, it might lead to another one that does. I think that's true for any design project!

HERE IN THE BLUE ROOM I HAVE USED MY MOSAIC TECHNIQUES IN MANY PLACES.

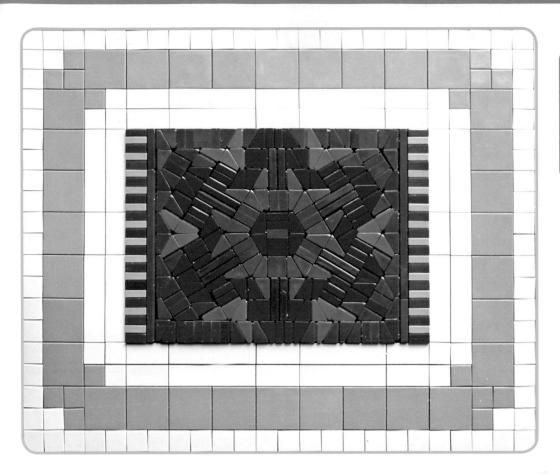

Building Tip

I sometimes use toothpicks or tweezers to push pieces into place. They're more precise than your fingers, and if a piece tips over it's much easier to pull it out.

Grandfather Clock

1

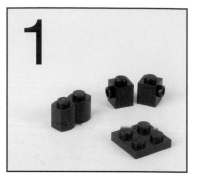

2

3

4

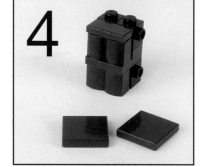

5

6

7

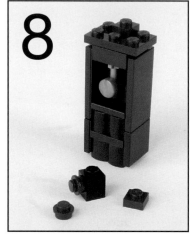

8

9

10

11

12

164

HERE ARE SOME COURTYARDS AND INTERIORS THAT USE MY MOSAIC TECHNIQUES.

WOW, YOUR COURTYARDS AND INTERIOR SPACES COMPLEMENT EACH OTHER BEAUTIFULLY. I WISH I COULD SEE MORE AMAZING ENVIRONMENTS LIKE THESE.

WELL, I AM A FAIRY, AND WISHES ARE MY SPECIALTY. GOOD LUCK WITH YOUR TRAVELS, MEGS. FAREWELL!

Full Steam Ahead

Carl Greatrix

Nickname: Bricktrix

Profession: LEGO Model Designer at TT Games

Nationality: British

Websites: *www.flickr.com/photos/bricktrix/*
www.brickshelf.com/cgi-bin/gallery.cgi?f=309654

THIS IS CORFE CASTLE—WELL, THE LEGO VERSION, ANYWAY. I'M STATION MASTER CARL.

WOW, KATIE'S MAGIC REALLY WORKED! YOU MADE ALL THIS? I'VE NEVER SEEN A FLOOR LIKE THIS BEFORE.

SOME AREAS OF CORFE CASTLE USE MODEL RAILWAY PARTS (LIKE THE GRASS AND THE GRAVEL), BUT ALL OF THE VEHICLES, BUILDINGS, AND PLANTS ARE MADE FROM LEGO PIECES. WOULD LIKE TO SEE SOME MORE OF MY TRAINS?

THAT WOULD BE LOVELY!

BRICKTRIX IS ONE OF MY FAVORITES, WHICH IS WHY I NAMED IT AFTER MYSELF.

Jinty Tank Engine

YOU WILL NEED TO PUT YOUR ENGINEER'S THINKING CAP ON FOR THIS BUILD—IT HAS A LOT OF WORKING PARTS. TAKE YOUR TIME AND STUDY THE INSTRUCTIONS CLOSELY. I RECOMMEND THAT ONLY THE MOST EXPERIENCED LEGO BUILDERS TRY TO TACKLE THIS MODEL.

1

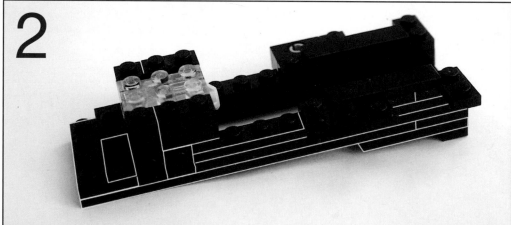

2

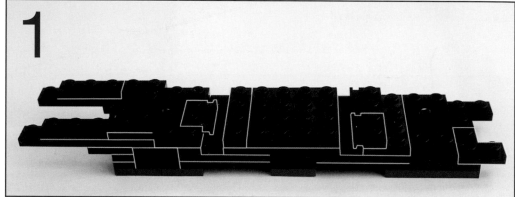

3

4

5

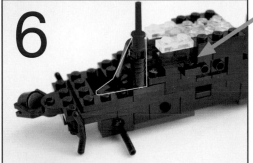

6

7

8

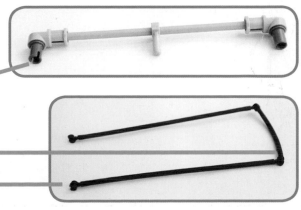

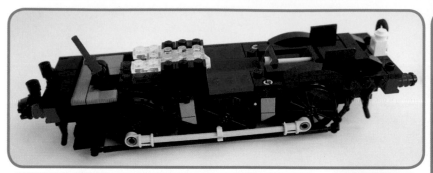

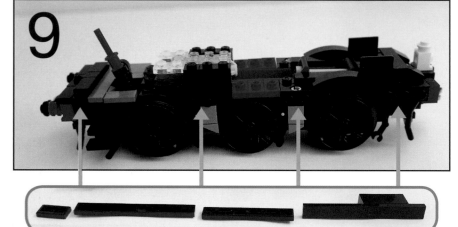

9

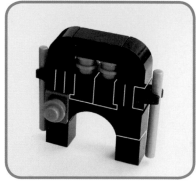

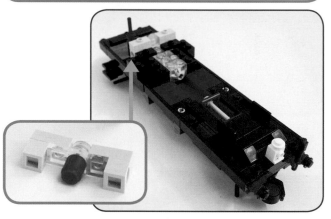

10

11

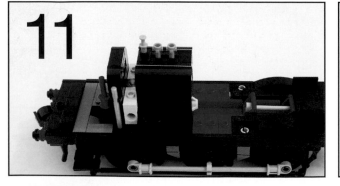

12

Building Tip
Set aside the assembly in step 12 for now. We'll need it later in the build.

13

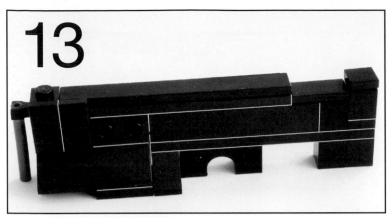

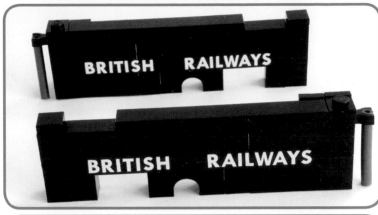

14

15

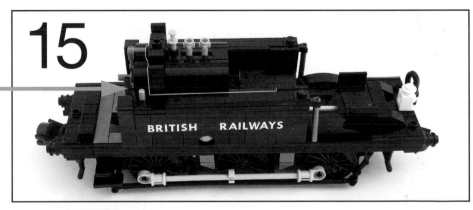

16

17

18

Building Tip
This very complex model is difficult to build. Carefully study the pictures and concentrate on building the small subassemblies correctly.

19

BRITISH RAILWAYS

BRITISH RAILWAYS

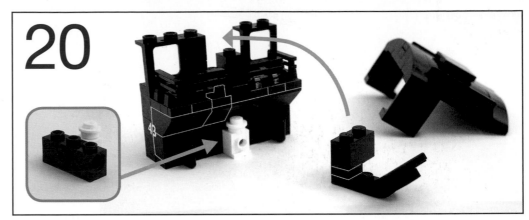

20

21

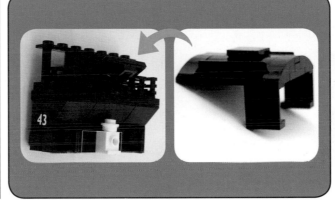

22

BRITISH RAILWAYS

British Railways 0-6-0, Fowler Class 3F, "Jinty" Tank Engine (in operation 1924–1967)

Train Features

Working brakes
(via cab brake lever)

Working lit firebox
(light brick trigger via boiler)

Removable cab section
(access to the brake lever)

WELL, YOU WERE RIGHT, CARL, THAT WAS A DIFFICULT BUILD. IT DOES GIVE ME SOME GOOD IDEAS FOR BUILDING ON TRAIN TRACKS!

YES, I LIKE A GOOD CHALLENGE! HERE, I'LL SHOW YOU MORE OF CORFE CASTLE STATION.

Corfe Castle Station

BUILDING JOURNAL

Carl uses stickers to great effect. He cuts the edges off official LEGO sticker sheets and uses them to make window frames and even stripes on some of his vehicles. He's also used his own printed stickers to create unique and accurate LEGO models. These techniques are a great way to make models look a lot more realistic, but it takes practice to get them right.

Building Tip
Think about your passengers. For example, build a bridge over the tracks so they can walk to the other platform safely. A railway station needs more than trains, too. Check out the other vehicles that workers and passengers might use.

BUILDING THE SURROUNDING ENVIRONMENT IS A GREAT OPPORTUNITY TO ADD IN SOME FUN DETAILS.

I'LL SAY. HEY, IS THAT SUPERMAN?

NO, THAT'S JUST BOB. HEY, BOB, YOU'VE PUT YOUR UNDERWEAR ON LAST AGAIN!

OF COURSE, YOU DON'T HAVE TO BUILD JUST STEAM TRAINS. YOU CAN BUILD DIESEL ENGINES OR EVEN ELECTRIC LOCOMOTIVES IF YOU WANT TO.

BUILDING JOURNAL

Carl's trains gave me lots of great ideas. They have working lights, actually move, and are really powerful. When I get back to the Idea Lab, I'll try building something that runs on rails. I'm just not sure it will be a train like his!

THIS IS MY PRIDE AND JOY, A MODEL OF THE *MALLARD*. IT HAS HELD THE WORLD SPEED RECORD FOR STEAM LOCOMOTIVES SINCE 1938. WHAT AN ACHIEVEMENT!

I'VE ALWAYS LIKED THE STEAM ENGINES FROM THE GRAND DAYS OF TRAVEL, AND THIS ONE IS BRILLIANT! I WONDER WHAT ELSE STEAM POWER CAN ACCOMPLISH. BRICKBOT?

No problem. Beaming you to a new location now, Megs.

BYE, CARL. THANKS FOR EVERYTHING!

GOOD-BYE, MEGS. WHAT A PECULIAR LADY. QUITE NICE, THOUGH.

Steampunk

Sylvain Amacher

Nickname: Captain Smog

Profession: Graphic Designer

Nationality: Swiss

Website: *www.flickr.com/photos/captainsmog/*

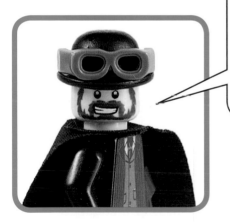

LET ME INTRODUCE YOU TO THE *ARMS OF TOIL*. I CREATED IT TO HELP MEN CARRYING HEAVY LOADS. YOU WILL BE USING A LOT OF SMALL PARTS TO BUILD IT; FOLLOW THE ARROWS AND YOU SHOULD BE SUCCESSFUL. WE SHALL BEGIN WITH THE CORE OF THE EXOSKELETON: THE BOILER.

Arms of Toil

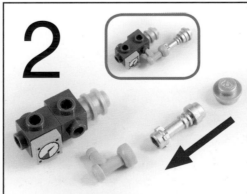

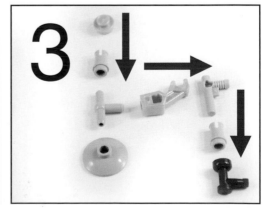

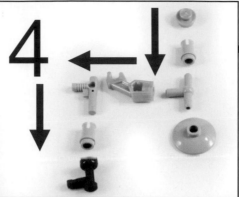

4

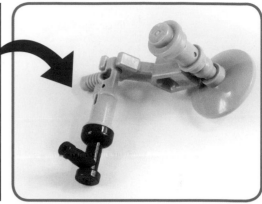

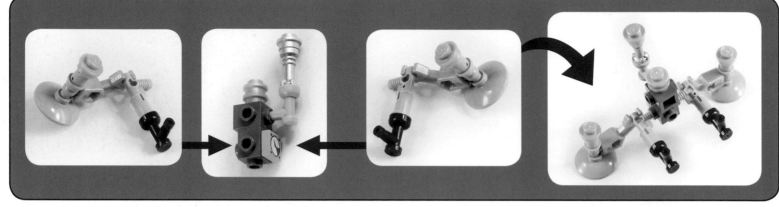

5

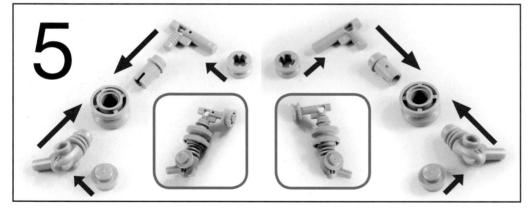

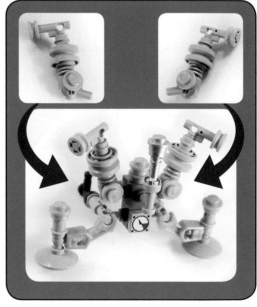

6

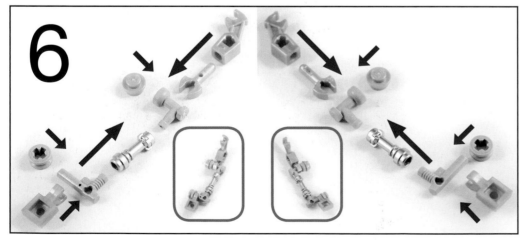

Building Tip
The color scheme is important. Gold, copper, black, brown, dark green, and dark red all help create the right Victorian feel.

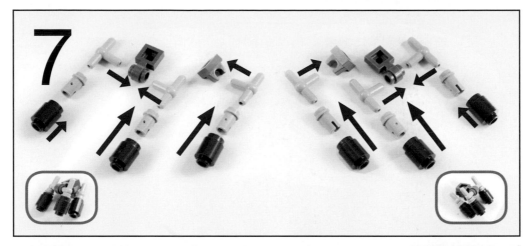

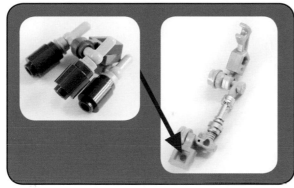

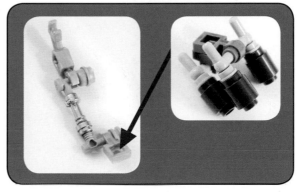

CONTRAPTION COMPLETED! THIS IS ONLY ONE OF MANY STEAM DEVICES YOU CAN CREATE. LET ME SHOW YOU SOME OTHER CONTRIVANCES.

HERE WE HAVE THE URBAN STEAM MONORAIL!
IT'S A VERY FAST WAY TO TRAVEL TO EXOTIC
DESTINATIONS. EACH CAR CAN TAKE UP TO EIGHT
PASSENGERS COMFORTABLY.

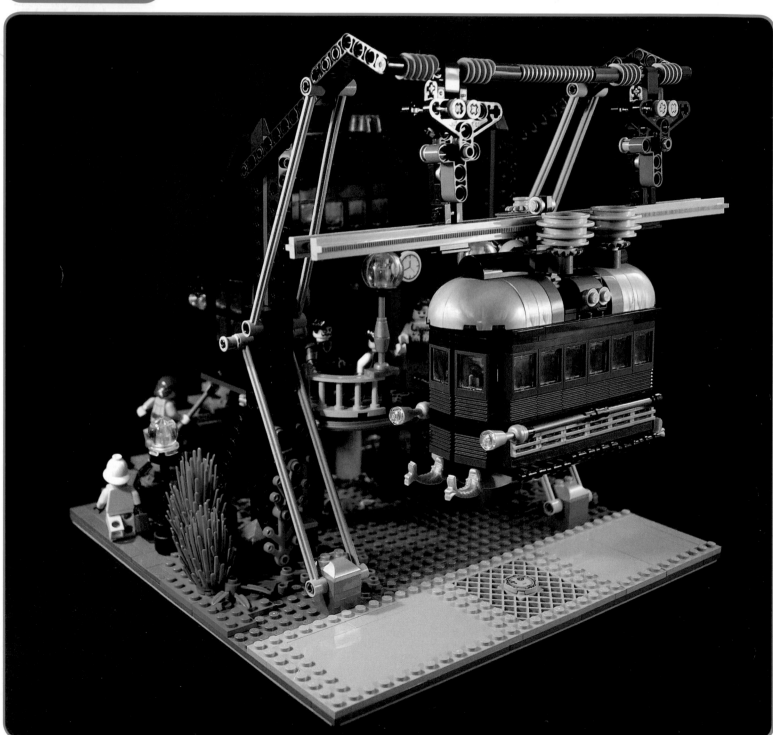

THESE ARE INDEED SOME CURIOUS DEVICES, MY GOOD SIR.

OF COURSE, I HAVE MY OWN DEVICE: THE TRANSPORT-O-LUX. IT ALLOWS ME TO EXPLORE INGENIOUS LEGO CREATIONS THROUGH TIME AND OTHER DIMENSIONS.

AHHH, THAT *IS* A HANDSOME DEVICE YOU HAVE THERE. IS IT POWERED BY THE ALMIGHTY STEAM TOO?

NO, GOOD SIR, 'TIS IMAGINATION THAT DRIVES THIS FINE CRAFT.

IMAGINATION, YOU SAY? WE'VE PLENTY OF THAT TO GO AROUND HERE! COME, MISS, LET US EXPLORE THE INFINITE POSSIBILITIES OF THE IRON LEGS.

The Iron Legs

SPIFFING, MY GOOD MAN. THESE ARE QUITE TALL CONTRAPTIONS, INDEED.

BUILDING JOURNAL

Steampunk seems like a really difficult genre to get right. It's part steam power, part clockwork, and part science fiction. I should look at some real steam-powered vehicles from the Victorian era and borrow some details from them. The metal parts are often painted bright colors to stop them from rusting, the machinery is metal cogs, and the delicate parts are made of brass. Steam engines need big boilers and have chimneys, too.

AH, BRICKBOT, MY CLEVER MECHANICAL WONDER!

INDEED, I AM, MY SHINY FRIEND! WHAT IS IT THAT YOU REQUIRE?

Megs? Can you hear me?

My syntax sensors detect that you must be in a steampunk empire!

I just received a message from someone named Katie that says, "Megs, I think you'll like this." She has attached some coordinates.

WELL, THAT IS AN UNEXPECTED TURN OF EVENTS. BEAM ME AT YOUR EARLIEST CONVENIENCE TO THOSE DISTANT COORDINATES. LET US DEPART POSTHASTE!

THANK YOU KINDLY FOR SHARING YOUR KNOWLEDGE, CAPTAIN SMOG. SADLY, I MUST TAKE MY LEAVE NOW FOR PARTS UNKNOWN! I WISH YOU FINE LUCK WITH YOUR FUTURE CREATIONS.

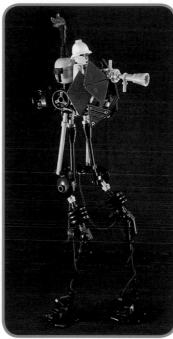

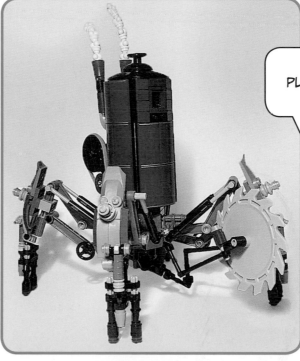

IT WAS MY PLEASURE, MILADY. BON VOYAGE!

189

A LEGO Legend

Daniel August Krentz

Profession: Retired LEGO Designer

Nationality: American/Danish

YOU MAY TRY BUILDING MY YELLOW CASTLE HOUSE IF YOU LIKE.

Thinking Tower

WOW! IT'S BEAUTIFUL!

WHY, THANK YOU, MEGS! I DO LIKE TO BUILD FANTASY LEGO MODELS.

I ALSO LIKE TO ADD DETAILS, LIKE DOOR HANDLES, FLOWERS, AND BANISTERS. THEY MAKE MY MODELS MORE REALISTIC.

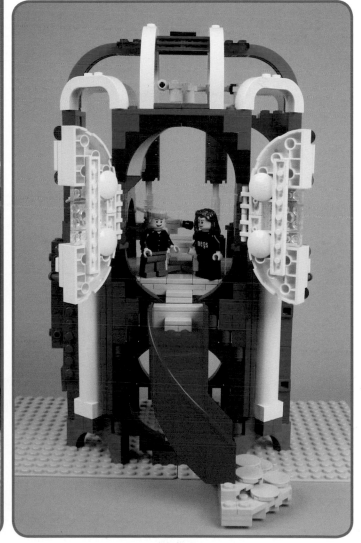

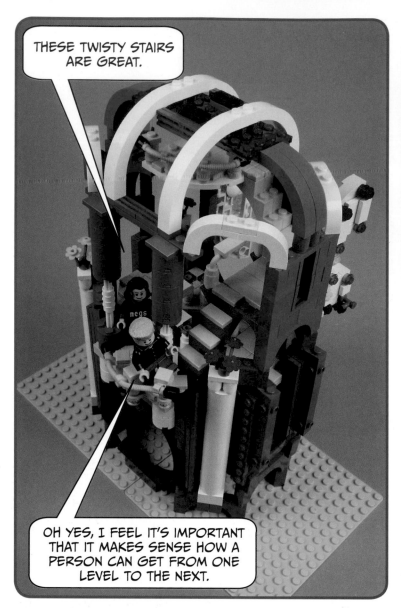

THESE TWISTY STAIRS ARE GREAT.

OH YES, I FEEL IT'S IMPORTANT THAT IT MAKES SENSE HOW A PERSON CAN GET FROM ONE LEVEL TO THE NEXT.

THESE ANGLED CORNERS ARE INTERESTING.

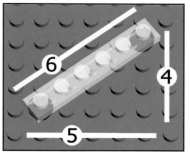

6

4

5

THAT'S LEGO GEOMETRY! A SIX-STUD ARCH WILL LINE UP IF IT IS TWISTED UNTIL IT IS FOUR STUDS UP AND FIVE STUDS OVER. THERE ARE QUITE A FEW WAYS BRICKS CAN BE PLACED DIAGONALLY, AND IT'S QUITE DIFFICULT TO BUILD LARGE STRUCTURES WITH THEM. I ENJOY THAT KIND OF CHALLENGE.

Building Tip

To figure out the diagonal possibilities of LEGO bricks, take a brick (or a plate) and put any 1×1 element on each end. Attach one end of the brick to a baseplate, and rotate it until it reaches a stud. Does it fit without being forced? Congratulations, you have discovered a usable building connection. To create a smooth surface between your connection points, cover the exposed studs with tiles.

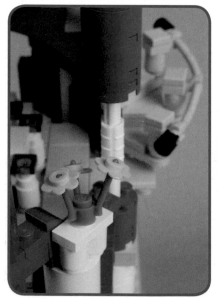

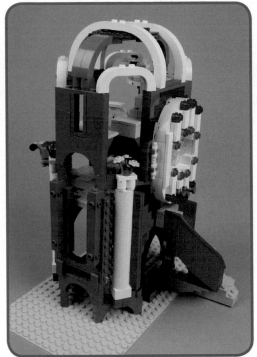

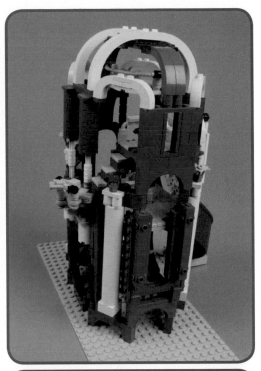

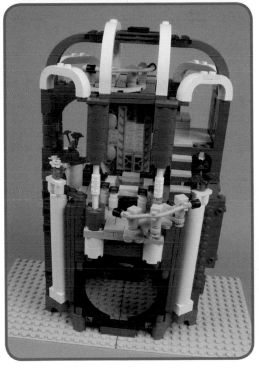

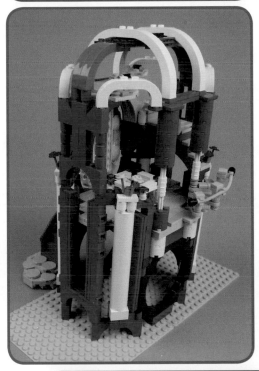

NOW COME WITH ME. YOU NEED TO SEE THIS!

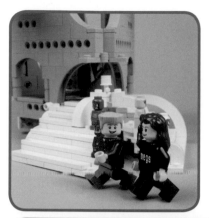
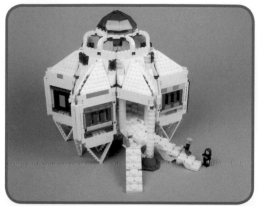

Idea Temple

THIS IS MY IDEA TEMPLE. ITS SHAPE IS BASED ON A SIX-POINTED STAR.

NEAT!

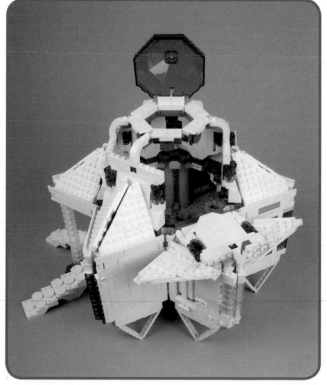

BUILDING JOURNAL

I can't really describe what it was like in the Idea Nexus. I don't even know how long I lay there. All of the places I had visited and all of the models I had seen suddenly merged together in my head. I felt my creativity levels boosted, and I knew I had to get back to my Idea Lab and Brickbot and start building.

THE END

(for now)

1  **Megan Rothrock**

Nickname: megs/megzter
Profession: Toy Designer
Nationality: American
Website: *www.flickr.com/photos/megzter/*

Thank you to all the wonderful and creative featured builders:

2  **Craig Mandeville**

3 **Are J. Heiseldal**

4 **Moritz Nolting**

5  **Jon Hall**

6 **Pete Reid**

7  **Peter Morris**

8  **Mark Stafford**

9 **Aaron Andrews**

10 **Mike Psiaki**

11 **Katie Walker**

12 **Carl Greatrix**

13  **Sylvain Amacher**

14  **Daniel August Krentz**